Developing Anti-Racist Cultural Competence

About the Author

Rehman Abdulrehman, PhD, is a Canadian Muslim of Zanzibari descent who works as a clinical and consulting psychologist. His work has spanned continents and cultures, with a focus on the intersection of mental health; diversity, equity, and inclusion; and leadership. Among the clients that Dr. Abdulrehman has supported to address diversity, equity, and inclusion are Google/YouTube, Mastercard Foundation, the Canadian Broadcasting Corporation, and the Government of Canada. He has developed and hosted a podcast, Different People, addressing difficult conversations on racism, and developed the Bias Outside the Box tool, which went viral, to help people begin a conversation with themselves about the biases they hold. Dr. Abdulrehman was also a TEDx speaker with his talk "Resolving Unconscious Bias," and his work has been recognized by the Society of Consulting Psychology for Excellence in Diversity & Inclusion Consulting. He is also an assistant professor with the Department of Clinical Health Psychology at the University of Manitoba and has held three visiting professor positions at Zanzibar University, the State University of Zanzibar, and Muhimbili University of Health and Allied Sciences, due to his development work in Tanzania. He was also the Chair of the Committee on International Relations in Psychology for the American Psychological Association (2015–2016). Dr. Abdulrehman's work has been recognized by the Society of Consulting Psychology for Excellence in Diversity and Inclusion (D&I) Consulting (2022).

Advances in Psychotherapy – Evidence-Based Practice

Series Editor

Danny Wedding, PhD, MPH, Professor Emeritus, University of Missouri–Saint Louis, MO

Associate Editors

Jonathan S. Comer, PhD, Professor of Psychology and Psychiatry, Director of Mental Health Interventions and Technology (MINT) Program, Center for Children and Families, Florida International University, Miami, FL

J. Kim Penberthy, PhD, ABPP, Professor of Psychiatry & Neurobehavioral Sciences, University of Virginia, Charlottesville, VA

Kenneth E. Freedland, PhD, Professor of Psychiatry and Psychology, Washington University School of Medicine, St. Louis, MO

Linda C. Sobell, PhD, ABPP, Professor, Center for Psychological Studies, Nova Southeastern University, Ft. Lauderdale, FL

The basic objective of this series is to provide therapists with practical, evidence-based treatment guidance for the most common disorders seen in clinical practice – and to do so in a reader-friendly manner. Each book in the series is both a compact "how-to" reference on a particular disorder for use by professional clinicians in their daily work and an ideal educational resource for students as well as for practice-oriented continuing education.

The most important feature of the books is that they are practical and easy to use: All are structured similarly and all provide a compact and easy-to-follow guide to all aspects that are relevant in real-life practice. Tables, boxed clinical "pearls," marginal notes, and summary boxes assist orientation, while checklists provide tools for use in daily practice.

Advances in Psychotherapy – Evidence-Based Practice, Volume 53

Developing Anti-Racist Cultural Competence

Rehman Abdulrehman
Clinic Psychology Manitoba, Private Practice, Winnipeg, MB, Canada
Lead With Diversity, Diversity Consulting Firm, Winnipeg, MB, Canada
Department of Clinical Health Psychology, Max Rady College of Medicine,
Faculty of Health Sciences, University of Manitoba, Winnipeg, MB, Canada

Library of Congress of Congress Cataloging in Publication information for the print version of this book is available via the Library of Congress Marc Database under the Library of Congress Control Number 2024931598

Library and Archives Canada Cataloguing in Publication

Title: Developing anti-racist cultural competence / Rehman Abdulrehman, Clinic Psychology Manitoba,
   Private Practice, Winnipeg, MB, Canada, Lead With Diversity, Diversity Consulting Firm,
   Winnipeg, MB, Canada, Department of Clinical Health Psychology, Max Rady College of Medicine,
   Faculty of Health Sciences, University of Manitoba, Winnipeg, MB, Canada.
Names: Abdulrehman, Rehman, author.
Series: Advances in psychotherapy--evidence-based practice ; v. 53.
Description: Series statement: Advances in psychotherapy--evidence-based practice ; volume 53 |
   Includes bibliographical references.
Identifiers: Canadiana (print) 20240299183 | Canadiana (ebook) 20240299191 | ISBN 9780889375154
   (softcover) | ISBN 9781616765156 (PDF) | ISBN 9781613345153 (EPUB)
Subjects: LCSH: Cultural competence—Handbooks, manuals, etc. | LCSH: Self-evaluation—Handbooks,
   manuals, etc. | LCSH: Anti-racism—Handbooks, manuals, etc.
Classification: LCC HM793 .A23 2024 | DDC 303.48/2—dc23

© 2024 by Hogrefe Publishing

www.hogrefe.com

The authors and publisher have made every effort to ensure that the information contained in this text is in accord with the current state of scientific knowledge, recommendations, and practice at the time of publication. In spite of this diligence, errors cannot be completely excluded. Also, due to changing regulations and continuing research, information may become outdated at any point. The authors and publisher disclaim any responsibility for any consequences which may follow from the use of information presented in this book.

Registered trademarks are not noted specifically as such in this publication. The use of descriptive names, registered names, and trademarks does not imply, even in the absence of a specific statement, that such names are exempt from the relevant protective laws and regulations and therefore free for general use.

The cover image is an agency photo depicting models. Use of the photo on this publication does not imply any connection between the content of this publication and any person depicted in the cover image.
Cover image: © Ian McCausland
Illustrations: Naomi Faber

PUBLISHING OFFICES

USA: Hogrefe Publishing Corporation, 44 Merrimac St., Suite 207, Newburyport, MA 01950
       Phone 978 255 3700; E-mail customersupport@hogrefe.com

EUROPE: Hogrefe Publishing GmbH, Merkelstr. 3, 37085 Göttingen, Germany
          Phone +49 551 99950 0, Fax +49 551 99950 111; E-mail publishing@hogrefe.com

SALES & DISTRIBUTION

USA: Hogrefe Publishing, Customer Services Department,
       30 Amberwood Parkway, Ashland, OH 44805
       Phone 800 228 3749, Fax 419 281 6883; E-mail customersupport@hogrefe.com

UK: Hogrefe Publishing, c/o Marston Book Services Ltd., 160 Eastern Ave.,
      Milton Park, Abingdon, OX14 4SB
      Phone +44 1235 465577, Fax +44 1235 465556; E-mail direct.orders@marston.co.uk

EUROPE: Hogrefe Publishing, Merkelstr. 3, 37085 Göttingen, Germany
          Phone +49 551 99950 0, Fax +49 551 99950 111; E-mail publishing@hogrefe.com

OTHER OFFICES

CANADA: Hogrefe Publishing Corporation, 82 Laird Drive, East York, Ontario, M4G 3V1

SWITZERLAND: Hogrefe Publishing, Länggass-Strasse 76, 3012 Bern

Printed and bound in the USA

ISBN 978-0-88937-515-4 (print) · ISBN 978-1-61676-515-6 (PDF) · ISBN 978-1-61334-515-3 (EPUB)
https://doi.org/10.1027/00515-000

Dedication

Despite feeling like I was in touch with my cultural identity, I did not realize just how much of my cultural self I had locked up in the back of my mind until my son came into my life. When I observed the impact of a White-centered world on him, I saw a conflict in identity early in his life, and in realizing that, I also came to be aware of how much of my own cultural self I had imprisoned, simply to ensure a greater sense of safety for myself, and a comfort for those from the majority culture. In the realization of the experience of my son, my approach to cross-cultural competency shifted, requiring that my academic training and experience begin to line up with my personal lived experience, as it too had critical importance in the understanding of what it meant to be cross-culturally competent. Lived experience, as I was learning from my son, was so critical to our understanding of how to work better with people we perceive to be different. This book is dedicated to you, Yousuf, for opening my eyes. And to my parents, who endured the onslaught of systemic racism against their cultural identities, to ensure their children gained the privilege of finding a sense of safety they did not and do not have in a supposed "multicultural" society. To my brothers too, with whom I learned alongside, with whom I survived cultural erasure through humor and wit, and with whom I consistently debate and discuss what our cultural identity actually is. To my family, all of you, I dedicate this book, a symbol of our survival in a world where racism and discrimination of all forms tried to erase who we were as a people.

Acknowledgments

Sincere acknowledgments to the dedicated psychologists who already do this work on cross-cultural competence and anti-racism, including but not limited to Drs. Derald Wing Sue and Monnica Williams. Thanks to Dr. Sonya Faber for her assistance with helping to translate my model of cultural and ethnic identity development into a visual model.

Contents

Foreword

If working in the area of diversity training and research for 20 years has taught me something, it's that teaching anyone anything about race, ethnicity, and culture is a hazardous minefield of hidden dangers. People tend to be very embedded in their own worldview and perspectives, and simply providing the facts is rarely enough to bring about a meaningful shift in thinking. The issue of race is perhaps one of the thorniest areas to navigate, as White people in Western cultures are socialized from birth to not see the advantages they gain from Whiteness. Likewise, people of color learn that pointing out racial inequities often engenders social punishment, and so they learn to keep quiet when not with trusted others. And when you assemble a group of people of different races, ethnicities, and cultures in one classroom, talking about these issues can be volatile. I have known many colleagues who endured classroom discussions that quickly devolved into chaos and became unmanageable – to the point where even the professor was left in tears (Faber & Williams, 2023). Teaching this material can be especially perilous for untenured faculty, as noted by Boatright-Horowitz and Soeung, whose 2009 paper on the matter is tellingly titled "Teaching White Privilege to White Students Can Mean Saying Good-bye to Positive Student Evaluations."

Fortunately, my own courses on diversity usually go quite well – which I attribute in part to learning from my prior disastrous attempts (yes, attempts plural) at teaching multicultural psychology at the undergraduate level. Consistent work in this area has resulted in classrooms where my students are respectful of me and each other, and they genuinely appreciate their learning experience. Nonetheless, there are few good resources for teaching clinicians how to be culturally competent. In the process of teaching this subject at the graduate level, I eventually realized that I would need to produce the course materials myself if I was going to deliver the class in the way I wanted. This led to me writing two books, one on eliminating race-based mental health disparities across settings (M. T. Williams et al., 2019) and a second to teach clinicians about how to manage microaggressions in therapy (M. T. Williams, 2020). I was able to make good use of both of these resources until moving to Canada in the summer of 2019 from the United States. Although my Canadian students still appreciated the book on microaggressions, the one addressing mental health disparities did not translate as well into a new national health care context. And it wasn't long before students were asking for materials that were Canadian grown, as anything from the US was too easy to dismiss as not relevant in a country that tends to view itself as a multicultural utopia.

This request was a symptom of an even more pernicious problem. Too many Canadians drank the multicolored Kool-Aid and adopted the belief that only the US has problems with racial prejudice. As such, the problem of cultural incompetence may even be worse in Canada than the US, because many Canadians look with disdain at their neighbors to the south and believe that they do not need to learn anything more. But in reality, research shows that Canadians are every bit as racist as Americans (Gran-Ruaz et al., 2022). In my work for the Canadian government, I saw this first-hand when I led a team of psychologists that interviewed federal employees of color across six different agencies. Every person we spoke to had disturbing stories to share about racism, hate, and loss of opportunity (OAG, 2023; Williams et al., 2023). So as a result of biases and huge educational oversights, most people are inept at interacting across race, ethnicity, and culture. And I'll go ahead and add religion to this list too, since religious traditions are largely shaped by culture.

But rest assured, in the US, training and education on how to navigate cultural differences is deficient as well. During my journey as a clinical psychology graduate student at the University of Virginia, there was a gaping hole in our educational treasure map – the absence of any formal course to help us learn to engage with clients from different ethnic groups. My department did not offer any diversity courses at all, and graduate students were shooed away from venturing into the school of education, the only place where a graduate course on multicultural issues might be lurking. Our clinical psychology faculty, in their infinite wisdom, believed they had all the knowledge necessary to mold us into superior clinicians and researchers. Yet you cannot pass on the wisdom you never had. These professors, who had never been schooled in the art of addressing diversity, were simply unable to equip us with the tools we needed to launch into this next crucial part of our careers. We were only trained to treat White Americans.

Fast forward to 2023. We are post–George Floyd, which sparked a global racial reckoning. Racism is real. People of color are suffering. Most of us are now waking up to the fact that we are clueless and only pretending to have multicultural skills where we actually have none. In my experience doing diversity training in the US, Canada, and internationally, I find that even seasoned, mature, and otherwise well-trained psychologists struggle to operate in a culturally informed manner. Thus far I have yet to give a talk where I did not have to spend the first half of my presentation giving definitions to common cultural terms so that we could all be having the same conversation.

This brings to me this excellent book written by eminent diversity psychologist, Dr. Rehman Abdulrehman, *Developing Anti-Racist Cultural Competence*, which I wish I had had as a resource years ago. *Cultural competence* in simple terms is the capacity to interact effectively, inclusively, and fairly with people from diverse cultural backgrounds. Although the definition seems straightforward, its execution and realization are intricate and challenging. Cultural competence must be understood as an aspirational goal. While we cannot ever reach it as a final destination, the journey is necessary, as it enables us to make progress toward having more effective, inclusive, and equitable interactions across differences.

In this context, we should consider cultural competence an ongoing voyage rather than a fixed endpoint. We are constantly evolving in our cultural competence instead of ever truly attaining it, because cultural competence is a dynamic, shifting, and constantly demanding lifelong endeavor. And as Dr. Abdulrehman points out in this book, over time, culture evolves, and when two different cultures come in contact, they both are changed. As such, we cannot simply decide to stop learning, which underscores the need for cultural humility. One of the things I most appreciate about this book is the emphasis on learning about our own biases to ultimately promote trust, openness, and understanding among the diverse people in our world. And the bonus is that as we learn about ourselves and how to interact with people who are different, we improve all our relationships. We become more kind, empathetic, and sensitive. We become better citizens of the world – the first step in healing the mental health of a society that sadly continues to inflict harm upon itself. As such, I plan to make this book required reading for all of my students.

As such, I am truly honored to have been asked to write the Foreword for this enlightening book on cultural competence. Even though I have written over 200 academic papers and now serve as the Canada Research Chair in Mental Health Disparities at the University of Ottawa, I never cease to be impressed by my esteemed and accomplished colleague. I have seen Dr. Abdulrehman on major media outlets with national leaders, cogently commenting on the most critical social issues facing Canada. He has also worked overseas to bring mental health care to developing nations, and he presented a compelling TEDx Talk about the struggle to teach his son his cultural values in the face of a Western society that does not always embrace different cultural perspectives.

Having witnessed firsthand the transformative power of embracing diversity and fostering an inclusive environment, I am proud to endorse this book. Dr. Abdulrehman's dedication to promoting cultural competence and his insightful approach to addressing the challenges we face in this ever-evolving world make him and his work an invaluable asset. His book not only provides essential knowledge but also serves as a testament to his own commitment to advancing our collective understanding and promoting equity.

Monnica Williams, PhD, ABPP
Canada Research Chair in Mental Health Disparities
University of Ottawa, ON, Canada

References

Boatright-Horowitz, S. L., & Soeung, S. (2009). Teaching White privilege to White students can mean saying good-bye to positive student evaluations. *American Psychologist, 64*(6), 574–575.

Faber, N. & Williams, M. (2023). The intersection of race and femininity in the classroom. *Frontiers in Psychology: Gender, Sex and Sexualities, 14*, Article 1139320. https://doi.org/10.3389/fpsyg.2023.1139320

Gran-Ruaz, S., Feliciano, J., Bartlett, A., & Williams, M. T. (2022). Implicit racial bias across ethnoracial groups in Canada and the United States and Black mental health. *Canadian Psychology, 63*(4), 608–622. https://doi.org/10.1037/cap0000323

Office of the Auditor General (OAG). (2023). *Inclusion in the workplace for racialized employees* (Report 5) [Reports of the Auditor General of Canada to the Parliament of Canada]. https://www.oag-bvg.gc.ca/internet/English/parl_oag_202310_05_e_44338.html

Williams, M. T. (2020). *Managing microaggressions: Addressing everyday racism in therapeutic spaces*. Oxford University Press.

Williams, M. T., Faber, S. C., Abdulrehman, R. Y., MacIntyre, M. M., Harrison, T., Gallo, J. & Dasgupta, A. (2023, March 3). *The experience of racism by public service employees*. [Report commissioned by the Office of the Auditor General of Canada]. Government of Canada.

Williams, M. T., Rosen, D. C., & Kanter, J. W. (2019). *Eliminating race-based mental health disparities: Promoting equity and culturally responsive care across settings*. New Harbinger Books.

1

Description

1.1 Terminology

Dictionaries such as Oxford and Merriam-Webster often adopt words commonly used in everyday culture otherwise known as slang (e.g., pumpkin spice, yeet, Galentine's day), offering them legitimacy. Specifically, words and phrases from marginalized cultures have also been incorporated into these dictionaries, as elements of some experiences can best be described only by those cultures and by the people from those cultures who have unique worldviews and experiences. Words like "side hustle" (from the Black American community, reflecting the need for additional jobs or economic endeavors to create economic equity not typically afforded to the community), "coconut" (a person of color who is brown on the outside but has given up their culture to be White on the inside), and whitewashing (first used by Wiley A. Hall in the *Afro-American Star* in 1997, to denote Hollywood's removal of the perspective and presence of people of color in film; Helliger, 2022).

When the dominant culture does not acknowledge the presence, let alone represent the experience, of people of color and those from nondominant communities, it is difficult to rely on White people to explain the nuances of the experiences of these communities. This book will include both terms that are well known in professional circles, as well as terms and phrases developed by and used colloquially by communities of color, which reflect their cultural experiences as marginalized people in Western countries. Definitions and implications of these terminologies will be addressed as they are brought up in the book.

The words themselves reflect the challenges that many people of color face as cultural entities in the midst of a world and society where the standard set cultural expectation is White. And furthermore, the cultural challenges faced by many nonracialized or White passing people who come from Eastern cultures (e.g., some Arabs or Balkan Europeans) in a culturally dominant White world, where standards of culture are based in a Western White world rooted in colonialism. Each of these words or terminologies reflect the challenges faced by people of color in a White or Western world. Words like "coconut," "banana," or "Twinkie," "Oreo" (and even the exaggerated "double stuffed Oreo"), and "apple," reflect the ideology of lost cultural roots where someone can be one color on the outside, while inside they are culturally White. The terms "ABC" (American-born Chinese) or "ABCD" (American-born confused Desi) speak to Asian people losing culture to adopt Western or White culture in lieu of their own or even a healthy integration of both. The slur "Uncle Tom" refers to Black people who are humiliatingly subservient to White people, and reflects the pressure some people of color may face to defend, stand up for, and manage White interests against their own community of people, out of fear of being marginalized themselves. The term "fresh off the boat" refers to people of color who are not acculturated into White cultural dominance, but also highlights the pressure to conform. As does the almost opposite term "model minority," a phrase describing people of color who do as they are told by White culture, and who succeed by keeping their head down, not making waves, hoping to achieve the "American Dream." All these terms reflect cultural challenges of people of color, that are not always centered in our engagement cross-culturally. Yet they highlight a significant conflict and the presence of racism in nondominant cultural groups, who are not White. And based on that conflict, I will also introduce a term of my own, "psychological checkpoint," in Section 4.12, that discusses how in everyday society, it is not uncommon for people of color to have to pass through random psychological checkpoints, at the behest of White people, where they must confirm allegiance to political beliefs and ideologies, that advantage White people over people of color, in order for them to be granted access to services and everyday discourse and exchange of ideas.

I will address the topic of cross-cultural skills and development of those skills from a viewpoint that centers the perspectives and experiences of people of color in Chapter 6, and from an understanding of the terminology outlined above, throughout this book, but specifically in Chapters 4, 5, and 6. Furthermore, this book addresses these skills as something any professional must develop, rather than solely addressing health and mental health professionals, and I believe the responsibility for change lies in all professionals of all ethnicities and cultures.

Remember that learning about and being aware of these colloquial terms does not mean you can liberally use them yourself, particularly if you are not from the community they target. For example, if you are White and you call someone an ABCD, an Uncle Tom, or an Uncle Tom you will be very insulting. The same goes for terminology that is meant to be positive. So, for example, a White woman professional calling her Black woman client "girlfriend" can also be offensive because it can unintentionally create a mockery of cultural language and/or suggest an equality of privilege that does not exist. This may change with friendship and familiarity, in the same way that a romantic partner can call someone "sweetie pie" but a colleague cannot. Being aware of colloquial terms allows you to be aware of the experiences of people of color, but does not allow you to use them casually. But more descriptive terminology that describes an experience, such as model minority or psychological checkpoint, can and should be more broadly used to describe experiences of people of color when working with them professionally to better describe their experiences. Keep in mind that the client may not be aware of such professional terminology, so it is still better to describe the experience and query about it, before labelling it.

1.2 Overview

1.2.1. What This Book Is Not

In attending a very important and sensitive medical appointment about 10 years ago, I was greeted by an alert young resident, eager to do a good job. In her enthusiasm, one of the first things she said was, "Good to meet you. How are you liking Canada?" This medical resident was friendly, enthusiastic, and, I suspect, well intentioned. I wanted to assume, given her profession, that she was meaning to be sensitive to life experience and to be inclusive, ensuring newcomers felt welcome – except that I was not a newcomer. Had her assumption been correct – that I was a newcomer – then her intention would have been achieved; however, in this case it did the opposite. The error was in the assumption and would still have been a problem if I was a newcomer, because in either case the assumption was that because I was not White, I was not local. And though unintended, and though I am sure this resident would never assume to espouse such beliefs, the belief that determined this assumption and related behavior reflected racist ideologies; in this case that people of color are not local. For me, this assumption of my being foreign (though in itself, it should not reflect any offense) removed from me, my entire life experience and sense of belonging where I lived. It removed my childhood experiences growing up in Winnipeg, my relatability to my peers, my years of professional contribution dedicated to improving the community I lived in, which included people who looked like her, and made me feel that I did not belong. Ultimately, her assumptions made it impossible for me to fully trust her.

Though I did immigrate to Canada as a child, I had spent the vast majority of my life in Canada. A large sense of my belonging, identity, family, and work is tied to this country and the city in which I live. For somebody to make an assumption about my cultural experience, due to my name or the color of my skin, removes my sense of belonging, and it feels like an injustice because I am not seen for who I am, nor am I given the chance to be the author of my own social history in a medical setting. If a medical practitioner could make assumptions about my social history, what other assumptions might she make about me in my medical care? The assumption also adds to the power imbalance that is inherent in a patient–provider relationship. And in this case, it certainly distracted me from the health issue at hand. A single statement made her, and not me, the author of my experience (Illustration 1).

This medical resident's good intentions of attempting (or assuming) cultural competence backfired. Her biases (conscious or not) of what newcomers looked like, impacted her behavior and as a result, her patient care. Her focus was on assumed difference, instead of attempting empathy or understanding, and in this case, she failed in her medical responsibility. Though some of us may have already assumed her to be White (which she was), it is important to understand that the dilemma of bias impacts people of all ethnicities, immigration statuses, genders, etc. (Abdulrehman & Clara, 2023). And furthermore, the issue of cross-cultural competence is not simply

Illustration 1.

a Black and White issue, which suggests that the responsibility of developing culturally competent skills lies on all of us, not just on White people. When our understanding of cross-cultural work becomes dichotomous, or sustains a presumption that because we have understood one person, we can clearly understand those who look similar to them, we risk failing at our best efforts to be truly democratic in our supposedly pluralistic world.

1.2.2 This Is Not a *National Geographic* Read

What has frustrated me the most about the concept of cross-cultural competence is that many people, regardless of what profession they are in, approach it from an anthropological perspective. We interpret people to be different from who we are, and as a result, we approach them like we are people at a zoo. We learn about them and who we believe they are, in isolation from their interaction with us, missing the fact that interactions and relationships are like chemical reactions. The irony is that it's like we are looking into a fishbowl not recognizing that we are fish ourselves. It's a ridiculous concept to think about us examining people, as if we are not people ourselves. To me, the concept of cross-cultural competence is *not a National Geographic* window into places across the world. It is not about learning about a specific number of discrete cultures that do not intersect. Doing so would cause us to perpetuate concepts of orientalism, colonialism, and racism. This book does not approach cultural competence in that way.

Simply focusing on the differences between different groups of people perpetuates the myth of race and stratification by race. Cross-cultural competence that merely focuses on difference versus similarity, and on empathy for humans based on their experiences, is an approach that increases disparity racism and xenophobia and results in a lack of empathy and relatability. The simple fact that we do not treat the differences between subgroups in White communities (e.g., the White queer community, White people with disabilities, White Europeans) in the same anthropological sense as people of color suggests a problem in how we approach cross-cultural engagements. With differences between White communities, we strive to integrate the learning of differences as simply a better understanding of our own community, but with people of color, it feels like we are studying an entirely different species, needing to understand what feels like grossly different worldviews, when in fact, we sometimes lack the empathy and the motivation to see the challenges faced by people of color due to systemic marginalization.

To me, this book and the concept of cross-cultural competence, are more about ourselves than they are about the other. It is about how we better understand ourselves, the biases we carry in how we interpret those we perceive as different – their behavior and worldview – and how that perspective can impact our ability to truly understand a worldview different from our own as a human one – legitimate and valid, regardless of worldview or culture. From my perspective, cross-cultural competence is the ability to identify barriers to the ability to relate and empathize with people we perceive to be different, so we can help them like a fellow human, and a member of our community. In our understanding of our biases and the legitimacy of other worldviews, we can engage with others in a more equitable and democratic way that does not place ourselves above others, or vice versa. When we remove the barriers that come with bias and false and stereotypical interpretations, we are better able to relate and work with those we perceive to be different, from the common platform of a human experience.

> **Don't approach cultural competence like you're learning about animals in a zoo. You are always a part of the ecosystem**

1.3   Culture and Intersectionality

One of the key reasons I take the perspective that cross-cultural competence should focus on the practitioners' bias and worldview, is because doing it in the other direction seems improbable and silly. There are thousands of cultures and combinations of intersecting identities in the world. It becomes an impossible task to become an expert on the variations of intersecting cultural identities globally. Culture is also a fluid and organic construct that is ever changing based on social situations, politics, and even time. As an example, the Zanzibari culture my parents raised me with (here in Canada) is far different from the culture in Zanzibar today. Even the language I use is deemed by peers in Zanzibar and Tanzania as dated, or as one person said to me, "You speak like my grandmother." And yet, my culture here in Canada is both similar and different from that of a White Canadian with European heritage. And the experience and culture of my son will also shift in his experience based on mine.

Given the fluidity of culture, focusing expertise in just one area seems futile. It is our understanding of ourselves, and the concept of how we view and learn about others from cultural backgrounds different from and intersecting with our own that seems the more appropriate way to address the variation of human experience.

Even if we were to focus on a single international culture outside of our own, we would not be taking into account the social, economic, and political impacts on culture that leave it ever evolving. When working cross culturally in today's modern world, where migration and relocation is the norm, where the media and trends move things that range from music to value systems across the world in minutes, where families become increasingly intercultural and multiethnic, we must understand that cultures will mix, our identities will intersect, and as a result, intersectionality will become the norm.

Although I was an immigrant, I am also not a newcomer now, and still a Canadian fully aware of and engaged with many of the norms and practices present in my city and country. I live in a country where Christmas is celebrated by most, and though I understand it, it is not something I practice. For me, being Canadian and a Muslim means I attend prayer every Friday at a mosque and stop my work periodically throughout the day to pray. That cultural experience is a Muslim one, but for me it is also exclusively Canadian and has both distinct differences from the country in which I was born, and yet many similarities.

If I think of myself as an example of a client, at what intersection would I want to be viewed, or what would be the most accurate cultural intersection of my identity to be understood by any professional working with me? Zanzibar is a mixture of different cultures and ethnicities and, as a result of that, has developed its own unique culture. Should such a professional fall back on the cultures that made up Zanzibar? But I was born in Dar es Salaam, a mainland city in Tanzania, which also has its own unique culture – a mainland rather than an island culture (such as that in Zanzibar). Would that be the cultural perspective a professional should adopt when working with me?

Or should they approach me as a Muslim? And Muslims themselves have a diverse perspective of experiences and values and cultural experiences depending on the region of the world they grew up in or where their families may have originated. But then I moved to Canada. I consider myself a Canadian, and I have lived here most of my life. At which point do we need to be an expert on another culture to be well informed enough to work with people from diverse backgrounds? It becomes a ridiculous exercise in trying to learn about other people. So, what would be helpful? For me, it is important to be seen as a part of a society, to have similarities noted and not be seen as a foreigner. But it is also important for me to retain my cultural and ethnic identity and see myself as distinct. The challenge for any practitioner is to be able not to make any assumptions on either, and recognize that the challenge with me, would remain the challenge with any other White client, only the variables that made them distinct might differ. What would also need to be recognized for me, particularly in a therapy or health setting, would be the barriers I have experienced as a result of who I am.

We are always learning, and as professionals in any field dealing with people, our engagement with others provides us with opportunities to learn about different perspectives. In some professions, such as health and mental health, the need to understand social histories is critically important to understanding conceptualization of health and treatment. I believe many good professionals, psychologists or otherwise, generally take an open perspective in learning about the different life experiences of the people they work with. This allows them to apply their skills more successfully to the person they are working with.

I also believe that the ability to take a more open perspective regarding different worldviews is more difficult when professionals deal with individuals who are not from (or are perceived not to be from) dominant cultures (Owen et al., 2016). This includes people of color predominantly, or those who do not pass as White or coming from a White culture. Greater anxiety or fear of coming across as racist, or simply having flat-out unconscious bias, blind spots, and even racism, may also interfere with a typically professional process of getting an appropriate sense of your client from their perspective instead of your own. And thus the task of becoming cross-culturally competent requires some further detailed review as it will be explored in this text.

In referring back to the example of the medical resident who asked me if I was enjoying Canada, that single question demonstrated a clear misunderstanding of who I was, my sense of belonging to this country, this culture and she took a single aspect of who I was (and assumptions related to it) and made it the *only* aspect of my identity. Because she misunderstood me, my trust in her was grossly eroded.

We should consider how Derald Wing Sue, an expert in cross-cultural competence, emphasizes the importance of the client being the author of their identity and social cultural history. Sue (2019) defines "cross-cultural competence" as the "acquisition of *awareness, knowledge,* and *skills* needed to function effectively in a pluralistic democratic society (ability to communicate, interact, negotiate, and intervene on behalf of clients from diverse backgrounds) (page 65)" [emphasis from the author]. To interact and negotiate with, and intervene on behalf of, someone whose worldview is different from your own, you must first understand what they need and how and why they need it.

Cross-cultural competence seems simpler when viewed from this perspective. We all have the capability to learn about others; we do not need this book to focus on that. So then why do many people of color or those from nondominant cultures feel misunderstood (Constantine, 2007)? The dilemma comes in understanding the barriers to that understanding that are often systemic and entrenched in our thinking. Problems like colonialism, racism, and xenophobia are so normalized that they interfere with our ability to allow us to understand and accept others on their own terms.

Given, however, that people of color and those from nondominant cultural backgrounds face ongoing marginalization and racism, how is it that a well-meaning practitioner of any kind can develop the cultural awareness of such a broad range of people without anthropologizing them and being very limited in their scope? Advocacy becomes difficult to do if you do not fully understand what you're advocating for. In challenges like the one I (and the medical resident) experienced outlined at the beginning of this book, moving toward greater cultural competence is a necessary challenge, and one I hope this book and the following chapters will provide some guidance for.

1.4   What to Expect From This Book

This book will address the concept of cross-cultural competence from a *social justice* perspective. It will provide an overview of the common challenges facing many practitioners, and the clients they work with, to better identify barriers in the practitioner, and common issues in clients who come from communities of color or nondominant cultures. Issues of bias, racism, White supremacy, and even internalized racism will be addressed as common barriers to developing a better working and/or therapeutic relationship.

When considering cultural competence, as noted above, we tend to focus on learning about others. Though this information is important, it is not the essential information or skill behind the success of cross-cultural competence. Being cross-culturally competent means keeping an open mind, to identify your biases and to learn how to overcome those.

Models of cross-cultural competence do focus on learning about others, but first focus on learning about yourself and the barriers that you might carry, unbeknownst to you, that prevent you from understanding the differences between you and other people or understanding other people from a perspective that is from an egalitarian and equal perspective. It is imperative that clinicians have their client be the author of their own story, versus imposing your impressions of their story, your version of them, on who they are.

We have to learn to ask questions that do not imply that we know that person's story, learning about another culture and applying that bit of information across the board. This book will contain examples that are not just clinical or from therapy. There will be examples from everyday life and different sectors of work, because what we bring to therapy or our professional relationships are the engagements and experiences we have outside of the office or therapy room. Becoming cross-culturally competent cannot occur in the bubble of your work or therapy environment. Competence requires skills you must develop in daily life (M. T. Williams et al., 2023) and bring back into the therapy room or your work. Skills that are important in this book are not just for therapists, but for anyone in any line of work.

In my role as a clinician, professor, and diversity consultant, I have encountered many real-life scenarios that illustrate the challenges therapists and others committed to equity face. This book will combine research and real-life examples to help develop those skills for you, and how to engage in greater cultural humility.

Although the development of cross-cultural skills is critical for any work role, it is especially important in therapeutic and health settings, because vulnerability in these settings is at its highest and thus so is the need for trust. People from marginalized cultures experience an accumulation of small and big acts of racism, as described in the opening story of this chapter. Smaller acts, known as *microaggressions*, may not feel powerful as stereotypically overt acts of racism, but they accumulate and thus become deeply harmful. The concept of microaggressions will be reviewed too throughout several sections in this book, and in specific example scenarios.

Lastly, this book will address cross-cultural skill development through a social justice lens, helping put you and the people you work with on equal footing, especially if you come with privileges that can create chasms between the understanding of different worldviews. This egalitarian approach to therapy or any working relationship and relationship development is essential in cross-cultural skill development.

In summary, this book works at three levels: self-awareness, the therapeutic relationship, and the impact of both outside the therapy or work relationship.

2

Definition of Culture

Before we consider cross-cultural competency models, it makes sense to first consider the definition of culture. According to Merriam-Webster (n.d., Culture), "culture" is defined as "1a : the customary beliefs, social forms, and material traits of a racial, religious or social group," but also "1b : the set of shared attitudes, values, goals, and practices that characterizes an institution or organization" and "1c : the set of values, conventions, or social practices associated with a particular field, activity, or societal characteristic," and lastly, "1d : the integrated pattern of human knowledge, belief, and behavior that depends upon the capacity for learning and transmitting knowledge to succeeding generations." The words "food," "clothing," or "music" do not show up anywhere in that definition, and yet the vernacular understanding of culture typically has us consider those differences. Granted that food, clothing, and music may be derivatives or products of culture, the definitions above focus more broadly on beliefs, values, practices, and knowledge. And for that reason, focusing on components of culture such as food, clothing, and music, is like focusing solely on the window dressing of a home. Though they can make vital differences in appearance, they are not typically the foundation or the structure of the home in which people live, but sometimes can reflect individual values or preferences.

The definitions of culture are broad enough that they can and do reflect not just ethnic groups but social groups. In the same way that we have culture for ethnic and cultural groups, it is also important for us to recognize the culture of other groups, including such groups as a queer community, an organization, a professional community, etc. It is also important to realize that for groups that include people from dominant cultures (i.e., White people), efforts to understand those differences and be more inclusive tend to occur more easily without much confusion and without specific instructions needed regarding how to do so, than with communities of color. For example, though incredibly necessary, we note that business culture has moved quickly to include pronouns on emails (White people are reflected in the queer community), but we have not made the slightest movement in ensuring that people from nondominant cultural communities of color have their holidays and cultural celebrations acknowledged, with people offered paid days off as standard, nor have we incorporated those holidays into the calendars of a supposed multicultural or melting pot society (Pursaga, 2023; WinnLove, 2023). Or that understanding differences and how to engage with different professional or work communities comes about naturally, but we are stunted and anxious about engaging with people from communities of color when they are the majority.

2.1   Pluralism and Cultural Intersectionality

Derald Wing Sue's (2019) definition of cross-cultural competence (see Section 1.3 Culture and Intersectionality) clarifies that that competence rests on our ability to gain awareness, information, or knowledge about others (different from us) and the skills necessary to function with others in pluralistic societies. This would include how we communicate, engage, and interact with each other, but also how we can understand each other well enough that we may be able to negotiate for, intervene on behalf of, defend and support those who come from ethnic and cultural backgrounds different from our own. In diverse and pluralistic societies, the definition of culture becomes much more nuanced, as individuals may hold many different cultural perspectives and worldviews. With many cultures existing in a single society, and cultures being transported through work, migration, politics, and media, the concept of intersectionality now becomes the norm. We can no longer assume that someone's appearance, clothing, food, or choice of music reflects their full sense of their cultural and ethnic identity, and more importantly, their worldview. Cross-cultural competence is now more about how our values, and the values of those we work with juxtapose themselves with the values of a dominant society, and how those dynamics interact with any professional working relationship – in particular those with health and mental health workers. These worldviews, or beliefs, are critical contributors to how people feel (about themselves, others, and the world) and the decisions they make about how to engage with the world around them.

Any professional working in a pluralistic, diverse society will need to develop cross-cultural skills (specifically with people of color) because by the nature of the demographics of such a society, it will be cross-cultural. Not doing so will unwittingly promote the ongoing norm of a White-centered perspective of colonialism and racism, where White culture and White standards remain the unspoken norm. It is important to recognize that cultural presentation and worldview may not always coincide, and may require a more nuanced exploration in working with diverse clientele.

I will offer myself as an example. The clothing I wear (which was encouraged by my father and grandfather) tends to be very Western and, in particular, quite preppy: chinos, a button-down shirt, and my favorite, a wool or tweed jacket. Though from my appearance, people might assume I have assimilated into Canadian or Western culture, the reality is actually far more complex. The clothing I wear reflects an internalized colonialism, from my family who grew up in colonized Zanzibar. There, where the minority (the British) ruled and placed cultural expectations on a country different from their own, where the culture (including clothing in this case) determined interpretations of class, social status, and a sense of education and civility, many chose to adopt a British style of clothing. Though I was unaware of this influence for most of my life, I can see now the multigenerational impact on something I have always considered my own preferences. In fact, my sartorial decisions reflect the remnants and ongoing impact of colonialism and White supremacy. That said, I am also a strong advocate of justice, equity, diversity, and inclusion. I'm a practicing Muslim and consider myself well connected with my culture and the practice of my faith (Islam). And therefore, the clothing does not reflect my culture of origin, nor would it necessarily reflect many people's beliefs, values, and cultural and religious practices prior to colonization, and assuming so would be catastrophic for the trust of anyone working with me as a client. And yet, post colonization, this style of dress did become integrated as a part of my culture, and depending on where I was on my ethnic and cultural identity development, I may or may not have been open to having insight on this. The time, geographical region, and the politics and social circumstances of that time, had a clear impact on the culture of my family; some things they let go, others they maintained, for reasons that were healthy and sometimes not. And further to that, migration to Canada impacted my perceptions and my worldviews. Even my religious beliefs, thought to be rigidly held in another time and place, may have become more flexible in the space, time, and social circumstances I occupy today. Who I am cannot be interpreted by the clothing choices I make, the food I eat, or even the music I listen to. Nor can it be interpreted based on my country of birth or migration experience, but rather it must embrace the whole of my being. But still, assumptions about my identity, along with the identities of so many other people of color, continue to be made, quickly, sometimes unwittingly, and that can and does impact any professional and personal relationship I have.

I recall a student of mine, who worked with me, giving me a bottle of wine as a thank you gift, and when I turned it down, saying I did not drink, upholding Muslim values of abstinence from alcohol or recreational drugs, she was surprised noting, "I thought you were progressive based on how you behave." In this case, not just my clothing, but her perception of my not behaving in a way she perceived to be typical of Muslims – more specifically, her relatability to my engagement in the world (or her perception of my cultural manifestation), caused her to make a false assumption about my belief system and how I engaged in the world. Acting in her perception of the world, as a Canadian would, could not coincide with the fact that I could hold both sets of values and behaviors. Though giving and generous, her selection of a gift assumed I could not hold intersecting worldviews but needed to choose one. And intersectionality is the rule, not the exception when it comes to understanding cultural identity.

Though in this case, it was food that was involved in the cultural misunderstanding of my identity, the assumptions made were more tied to overall values and beliefs. Which reflects the underlying point that it is the values tied to life experiences and worldview that are important to understand. Values and life experiences are more important than what I choose to wear, in most circumstances. I barely eat the food that I ate when I was in Tanzania, as that is just a determination of geography and the availability of resources and sustenance. The ingredients for food changes, naturally by location, and shifts to what is available and convenient. Those issues are not cross-cultural ones for me, but in fact, minimize my sense of being and my identity, into tokenistic, carnival-type products. For me, someone who understood me in my intersecting identity, would see me as a Canadian of Zanzibari descent, but also a practicing Muslim (who by the nature of my own understanding of Islam being a moderate and balanced faith, consider myself fundamentally moderate in my belief) and whose languages (English included) reflect a broader understanding of the world around me. For me, someone who understood my intersecting cultural identity, would need to understand my values, as cross-cultural work is definitely about values and worldview, both of which are significantly influenced by experience.

The example of the student gifting me wine points to nuances in the discussion of food as a part of culture, where values, politics, and hate can become associated with food. In situations such as these, the cultural "window dressing" of food matters, because it is tied to broader issues of marginalization, hate, and sometimes complete cultural erasure. Take for example the blow East Asian restaurants suffered due to misunderstandings about East Asian food and the COVID-19 pandemic (Gover et al., 2020), where, due to racism and misunderstandings and assumptions about culinary aspects of East Asian culture, many populations around the world fully avoided those restaurants resulting in lost income and in some cases closure of restaurants that were livelihoods for families. An example of cultural appropriation is the de-Arabization of Palestinian food in Israel (Ranta, 2015) that co-occurred with an illegal occupation (United Nations, 2023a), where foods traditionally Palestinian and Arab (regardless of religious community), such as hummus and falafel, became rebranded as Israeli over the years following the forced displacement of Palestinians from Palestine in 1948 (Alhuzail et al., 2023). In all the examples above, the issue of food, reflects values, beliefs, and politics, all of which can be tied to the risk of ongoing marginalization. In situations such as these, food moves from being window dressing to the foundation of a home, but only because they are tied to broader issues of racism. And even though people from said cultural communities may not even eat said foods, the matter of their discussion reflects broader issues that can transcend local communities and international borders, which practitioners must be mindful of and be open to learning about.

2.2   Cross-Cultural Models

Some models for cross-cultural competence brilliantly separate cultures by dimension (Hofstede, 2011) and others by country (Meyer, 2016). Hofstede focuses on splitting cultures along the lines of six national dimensions of culture: power/distance, uncertainty/avoidance, individualism/collectivism, masculinity/femininity, long/short term orientation, and indulgence/restraint.

Meyers maps out cultures by country, and suggests that globalization leaves some people unprepared to find ways to communicate with clients and coworkers outside their own countries. Though the issues brought up by these models are not completely wrong, and there are variations in cultural expression and expectations, these models do the following: (a) they treat people outside the reader's perspective as an "other," treating the process as purely anthropological; (b) they focus first on the other person, or the client, before they do on the reader; (c) they do not address the ability of individuals to have understood dominant cultures, which is predominantly White culture (Gray, 2019; Okun et al., 2019), and we all understand the rules of such business; (d) issues related to racism, colonialism, and White supremacy are not addressed. The last is critically important, and largely the focus of this book. Interestingly, our ability to understand White cultures becomes far easier, and requires less complexity or insight, because of the centering of White culture globally. Complex models such as these aim to reduce the relatability between people, and exoticize what may be a pedestrian process if we simply are working to understand different perspectives and work from the perspective of equity.

Models such as those by Hofstede and Meyer, in my opinion, should warrant caution, and may be the reason why some reviews of cross-cultural competency training find limited evidence on the effectiveness in service delivery (Bhui et al., 2007). They focus, as mentioned above, on an anthropological approach, focusing on a scientific study of "the other." As noted by some, these models of "cultural competence" center Whiteness as the norm (Sufrin, 2019). And furthermore, they do not take into account how globalization has actually muddied the waters otherwise clearly delineated by historical borders where human interaction was minimized in the past by borders and boundaries.

It is fascinating to find ancient pottery techniques initially used in Mamluk pre-Islamic Egypt, in modern day China today (Vezzoli, 2019). There have been examples of some sense of historical colonialism, such as where the face of Alexander the Great has been found in art in the numerous cultures that his army and colony dominated, that speak to the vestiges of the values of a colonial culture that can be found in the cultures they dominated (Hughes, 2022; Palagia, 2022). Culture has always been organic and growing, and has become exponentially so the more our world has become globalized. The challenge, however, is to ensure the survival of cultures and to create space for nondominant cultures of people of color, and remove colonialist and racist presumptions of the superiority or standardization of a single cultural norm above all others. Doing so requires us to assume a model of cross-cultural competence that does not first focus on the other, but instead, on ourselves, as practitioners, examining how we can ensure that our own biases are not passed along or lead to violations of trust – or even worse, promote a greater internalized racism in the clients we work with. Any true working relationship requires trust and openness, which should lead to greater understanding of the dilemmas a client may face, and our ability to help.

2.3   Target Audience

When considering cross-cultural competence, we must consider who our audience is. In models such as the ones referenced above, experts focus on international work across borders, and therefore the thought of differentiating between people and cultures appears justifiable. These are, however, still largely colonialist (stratifying culture and people and focusing on learning about them without understanding ourselves), and they do not address the concept of globalization. These models are of little value unless one is working with clients from remote communities cut off from the rest of the world (and even then, one could argue that is largely improbable for most of the world today). For the majority of people living in diverse communities, cross-cultural work actually occurs locally, with people in their own communities. With increasing diversity across the world, and our greater understanding of differences between communities, cross-cultural competence is actually a core skill any professional should work on developing, to work better with those they already work with. In local diverse communities, models of cross-cultural competence that are dichotomous (your culture vs. my culture) are misleading, in that they divide more than they build harmonious functional working relationships.

2.4   Client Centered Models

Collins and Arthur (2010) provide a more comprehensive approach to developing cross-cultural competence, outlined by four primary components. This egalitarian model focuses less on borders, and is a more applicable model in any situation:

1. Identify your own cultural identity and worldview, including your own biases.
2. Understand the cultural perspective of your client.
3. Based on these two, you will be able to develop a culturally sensitive working alliance.
4. Address issues of social justice.

Mosher's model of cultural humility (Mosher et al., 2017) is similar, with a four-part framework that includes:

1. engaging in critical self-examination and self-awareness;
2. building a therapeutic alliance;
3. repairing cultural ruptures; and
4. navigating value differences.

Generally speaking, these models are most appropriate when working with people cross-culturally. Rather than "othering" the clients we work with, these models correctly identify the practitioner as a critical contributor to the working relationship between two people, and begins by first addressing the perspective of the practitioner. As outlined in the third component of Collins and Arthur's model and in Mosher's second point, the ultimate goal is of developing a culturally sensitive working alliance. This cannot occur if the relationship is hierarchical, assuming the supremacy of one party over the other (in this case, the practitioner). Though some cultures value professional hierarchies (getting advice from a professional), and these are therefore unavoidable, the supremacy of culture and ethnicity must be neutralized. Learning begins with the practitioner before there is learning about the client. The aim is not only to get to know the client and their worldview, but in particular, understanding how our own insight of ourselves as practitioners, including our cultural perspectives and worldview (including inherent and unspoken White supremacy), influences our ability to work with individuals different from us, in particular those from nondominant cultures in Canada the United States, and much of the Western world, without privileging Whiteness above all else. Any process of getting to know someone else, without realizing how we see others, has the potential to offend, demean, and remove a client's sense of belonging. Getting to know someone is not just about asking questions, but about which questions and when, and what information is necessary for you as the practitioner right away. For example, rather than starting on an equal footing, assuming there are differences, with the question "where are you from?" assumes difference, but also reflects stratification. When the person asking is White, it also reflects dominance and xenophobia, making the assumption that the White person is local and the person of color is from somewhere else; with someone who is local and belongs having more rights and permanence than one who is not. Getting to know someone to work professionally with them is also about ensuring trust. When we are unaware of our own worldview, including the biases we carry (e.g., assuming people of color are foreign), the questions we ask our clients (e.g., where our clients are from) and the way in which we engage with them (e.g., assuming differences before relatability) says more about us than it does about the strength of the working relationship.

2.5   How to Get to Know the Other Person Without Assuming

A common assumption made, and sometimes a question posed to people who are not White, is that they are not local (Canadian, American, Australian, European), and so they are asked where they come from. The assumption here is that they are not local, and that they are foreign. This attempt of getting to know someone, reflects more about the worldview of the person asking the question than it would produce actual information about the worldview and culture of the person being asked. And it underscores the importance of first having the practitioner reflect on their own worldview, their biases, and in particular, their blindness to the privileges they carry, as typically any work done cross culturally, with people of color in particular, will require a sincere attempt to overcome these biases. Otherwise, any attempt to get to know a person will risk being offensive, because questions will be filtered through our unconscious perceptions or our nonmindful perceptions of how we see the world. This insight can then also allow a practitioner to understand why they are asking certain questions, and what they will do with that information. Furthermore, how much of the need to ask comes from a need to compartmentalize their clients into a box, to assume greater understanding (which it does not).

2.6　Solutions

It is important to acknowledge that most of us understand full well how to get to know people without making them feel uneasy. We are familiar with social norms and decencies, and we are likely to ask courteous questions. However, due to privilege and our failure to appreciate the nuances of cultural differences and the consequences of racism, we are often less aware of how and when to ask about culture with people of color and those from cultural minority groups.

The thing that needs personal exploration on the side of the practitioner is the filter by which we ask questions: our own worldview, and our own biases and privileges. That is a piece that we need to pay attention to, because when we remove those barriers, we can ask questions at the right time, in a way that truly involves getting to know somebody, versus making assumptions about them. Or, without offending our clients, we can also create a space in which they will share the information they feel is relevant because they will not be threatened by the belief that they will be stereotyped and judged.

Consider the example of the medical resident who asked me how I was enjoying Canada. Her worldview and her understanding of herself in the context of a diverse multicultural world was flawed. Because of her lack of awareness, she made me feel misunderstood. I was being erased. It also left me in a position of choosing to explain this or defend this, if I was to be able to overcome a power differential, with the risk of it affecting my medical treatment. In either case, the burden remains on the person of color or the person from a nondominant culture. Practices such as this enforce marginalization and White supremacy. Assumptions or questions such as these relay the message that "I have been here longer than you have, and as such, am implicitly aware of more, and entitled to more, and my perspective is the measuring stick by which we will engage." What we do not recognize is we have assumptions about ourselves, and more than the assumptions about other people, we are revealing assumptions about our personal dominance and our cultural dominance. We must be thoughtful about our sense of permanence as a cultural or ethnic entity too, in relation to others, as it will reflect our sense of privilege, realized or not.

Greater dominance comes with greater privilege. It erases the experience of the person of color or person from a nondominant culture, and further internalizes trauma.

2.7   Intersecting Identities and Intersecting Cultures and Your Client

There are two critical issues we must consider from the Collins and Arthur model that are unique to a modern understanding of cross-cultural competence. The first is not explicitly mentioned, but I believe needs to be addressed, and that is *intersecting cultural perspectives* we have with our clients. The second is the issue of *social justice*.

The third component of the model – developing a culturally sensitive working alliance – is a stage in which we do not just learn about the client and their cultural perspective, but also realize where our cultural viewpoints may coincide with theirs. This allows us to fully recognize not only who we are, and who the people we work with are, but also where we may connect, relate, and empathize with the needs and rights of the people we work with as equally as we might advocate for our own rights. This would fit Sue's (2019) definition of cultural competence, a condition in which we can better advocate for, and negotiate on behalf of, our clients.

This is the precursor to the stage of understanding the need for social justice; it is the component that allows us to recognize that the need for basic human rights of individuals, despite our cultural perspective, is the same as ours. This middle ground is also the time in which our understanding of our biases, and how they impact our interpretation of how we see those different from us, our clients not from a common cultural experience, and allows us to decenter ourselves from the engagement we have with them, placing the needs of the client fully front and center of the working professional relationship, instead of unconsciously promoting a practice of White supremacy that centers our worldview, and ourselves as the professional, at the heart of the working relationship instead of the work we should be focusing on – to help the client.

Understanding that most clients we work with, who may appear to come from different cultures, are actually just members of our own community, helps us also understand that we will share many aspects of culture. Approaching the concept of cross-cultural competence from the perspective that clients are mostly international or exotic to us, reduces the common ground we may share with them – their identity. This makes our own cultural perspective the measuring stick by which we assess what is appropriate and normal. Yet, even if we were to work with people who are newcomers to our community or if we were doing work internationally where we are transplanted into other cultures, as noted previously, media, politics, and the social climate of the current world have created a shared global culture in which many phenomena are shared, creating a common footing between practitioner and client. That does not mean we assume all perspectives are the same, however; rather it also means we start with what's common and then learn about differences, instead of assuming the differences are real, and then consider how our skills can be applicable or adaptable, or thrown out entirely, when working with a perspective that does not fit our own worldview.

Without the attempt or insight to identify assumptions (or biases) about who we are culturally, there will be an increased chance that trust with the client will be lost, and any attempt to begin to understand the client culturally will be significantly decreased.

And so, although models of cross-cultural competence may vary in focus, ranging from understanding cultural perspectives to social justice, the issue of identifying one's own biases is critical to any process of cross-cultural competence – specifically, understanding the common cultural ground between the client and practitioner.

2.8   Social Justice

According to an IPSOS poll of Canadians (IPSOS, 2020), 28% of Canadians have experienced overt racism. When 29% of all Canadians identify themselves as Indigenous or people of color (Statistics Canada, 2021), this informs us that the prevalence of racism, though believed to be largely resolved, by those who do not experience it, really is not.

Haeny et al. (2021) define racism as

> a system of beliefs (racial prejudices), practices (racial discrimination), and policies based on individuals' presumed race, that operates to advantage those with historical power in most Western nations including White people in the US and Canada. In the US and Canada, race operates as a social caste system used to categorize people based on shared physical and social features. Even though an individual may be a racialized minority or Indigenous person they can still harbour racism. This is because our culture of racism affects all who have been socialized within it from childhood, and eventually racist thought patterns seem normal (M. T. Williams, Faber & Duniya, 2022, p. 18)

Understanding racism is a critical part of cultural competence

Williams (2020) reviews the impact of racism in numerous areas of global society and notes that in prospective studies worldwide, everyday discrimination predicted a number of poor outcomes, including the impact on common mental disorders in UK migrant and ethnic groups, loneliness in Canadian new mothers, poor adjustment after childhood trauma in Sierra Leone, and alcohol-related problems in American college students. She also discussed a nationally representative US longitudinal study of older adults, spanning two years, and found that everyday discrimination had stronger negative effects than major discriminatory events, especially on emotional health. In addition to mental health problems, everyday discrimination was found to predict increased inflammation, a risk factor for future cardiovascular disease; memory decline in older adults; chronic conditions such as heart disease, pain, and respiratory illnesses in Asian Americans; and low infant birth weight in African American women. This list is not exhaustive but clearly denotes the serious impact of racism on health and well-being. The quality and volume of the evidence is high that everyday discrimination contributes to stress experienced by people of color that can measurably worsen mental health and contribute to chronic illness, if not cause these problems in their own right.

M. T. Williams and colleagues (2018) have explained how the cumulative effects of racism can even lead to posttraumatic stress disorder (PTSD). According to this model, predispositions of vulnerability, such as epigenetic risk factors from historical or cultural trauma or racial oppression, set up a stress base, which is exacerbated by cumulative experiences of overt and covert racism. If individuals are the targets of racially traumatic events, they will experience emotions associated with this event, such as shock, fear, or anger. Further, if these experiences are invalidated, these individuals may develop symptoms of PTSD, such as intrusive thoughts, avoidance, hypervigilance, and negative changes in mood and cognitions. Finally, due to institutional racism and barriers to treatment, professional help may not be accessible, which maintains or worsens the symptoms of PTSD. This could take the form of lack of awareness by health care professionals and their discomfort with addressing issues of race, leaving PTSD from racism untreated (M. T. Williams et al., 2022).

Racism and systemic racism and historic colonialism, understandably then, have a significant impact on cultural and ethnic identity. When considering the example of my own family mentioned earlier, in the same way that our family chose to adopt a more British style of dress (living under colonial rule in Africa), these pressures impact who we are, how we see ourselves, and our cultural and ethnic identity. This view of ourselves, as people of color and from a nondominant culture, is also fluid, and can change depending on our life circumstance and insight, but the fact remains that it is difficult to disentangle cultural identity from the experience of marginalization, and so the issue of social justice is often discussed and becomes the center of many models of cultural competence (Buchanan & Wiklund, 2020; Collins, 2017, 2018, Collins & Arthur, 2010; Dollarhide et al., 2021; Goodman, 2013; Flores et al., 2014; Osanloo et al., 2016; Sue et al., 2018; Ratts, 2015). For this reason, this book will not address the skill of beginning to understand another person from a different cultural perspective from a perspective of data gathering, as it is something most are capable of. Rather, it will focus on how to obtain that information in a socially just way, with a focus first on the practitioner, developing a more egalitarian and just method of cross-cultural understanding, keeping trust as intact as possible.

Though the issue of social justice will be addressed in more depth later, it is my opinion that any process of cross-cultural competence in today's world begins with a strong understanding of the importance of social justice and the role of the practitioner in sustaining it, before putting the focus of difference first on the client. This approach decenters a dominant culture. The model of Collins and Arthur (2010) along with those of others (Sue, 2019) discuss the necessity of beginning to understand the practitioners bias first. In decentering the process of engagement, not just focusing on what is wrong with or how we can help the client, we focus on how our worldview and assumptions can negatively impact the engagement or treatment process.

To advocate for somebody, you truly have to have a nuanced understanding. In the same way it is difficult to lay out a meal for people with a vegetarian or vegan diet without exploring our understanding of what those terms mean, and what foods have animal by-products in them (remember it is values that determine this choice), and thus that attempt to make people feel welcome at a dinner is likely to be at greater risk of failure. For example, many people do not know that many gelatin-based products in Canada and the US (such as gummy candy and jelly, and even the frosting on certain cereal products) are made from animal by-products. Not maintaining a vegetarian or vegan diet would leave us blind to the circumstances of that diet, and put at risk the trust those people might place in us when coming for dinner. In a similar fashion, our understanding of issues of marginalization, racism, and xenophobia, are likely to be very restricted if we do not experience those ourselves, leaving us at risk of failing to build a culturally competent understanding of those issues.

2.8.1   What Social Justice Has to Do With Cross-Cultural Competence

As referenced above, given that nearly one in three Canadians are Black, Indigenous, or people of color (BIPOC), and nearly a third of the population has experienced overt racism in the past year, the understanding is that being a BIPOC person is tied to the experience of racism. In the same way, expressing one's identity and culture are also prone to discrimination and so, it is very difficult to remove the experience of racism from the cultural experience of being a person of color or somebody from a cultural community. In the same way that White supremacy is tied to the history of White people, and privilege is tied to the experience of being White, so is experiencing racism tied to people of color. It does not matter that this fact makes us feel uncomfortable, nor that many people today may be against the idea of racism, the statistics and personal experiences of BIPOC people confirm it is still a prevalent social issue today. Ignoring this in any professional relationship does not make it go away, in fact it increases the chances it may be perpetuated in the professional relationship, removing any chance of a culturally sensitive working alliance.

Even though they do not want it, people who come from marginalized communities, experiencing racism and marginalization and xenophobia will have that as a part of their identity, too. I cannot say to women, we can talk about being a woman without talking about sexism, because our world has been defined by patriarchy. How is it possible that I can talk about what it is to be a woman without experiencing sexism? I cannot say to gay people that we can talk about gay culture without addressing heteronormative standards of living. In the same way, we cannot remove the experience of racism when we are working with people of color.

It is this type of review of our own worldview and biases as practitioners that is needed through a social justice lens, as a necessity, and this binds social justice with cross-cultural competence. If you are not aware of the privilege that you sit with and the bias that it produces, then you will treat your clients accordingly. Without this review, *Whiteness*, including White culture, becomes the measuring stick by which we compare clients who are not White, or who do not come from White culture. Whiteness is what we will continue to measure experiences by. But what makes us believe that our perspectives, and, in some cases, White supremacy is the ruler by which the experiences of others should be measured?

It is critical to understand that the issue of reviewing our biases is not a task reserved strictly for White practitioners. Internalized perspectives of racism can occur regardless of ethnicity or culture. For those practitioners who are people of color, a further discussion of ethnic and cultural identity development and internalized racism will occur later in this book (see Section 4.2.). That section is meant to be focused on practitioners of color, and they should consider how these issues impact them and perhaps cause them to perpetuate racism due to their own internalized racism.

2.8.2   Social Justice, Trust, and the Therapeutic Relationship

A classic research study (Horvath & Symonds, 1991) confirmed that the most predictive factor for a positive therapeutic outcome was the strength and quality of the therapeutic relationship between the client and practitioner. However, that methodology only accounts for 10% of the success of psychotherapy. It is clear that a sense of trust is a critical factor necessary for a successful working relationship in therapy, and in numerous other works, outside of therapy settings as well. This speaks to what trust offers to people, that when we have trust, it redefines acceptance and the negative self-perceptions that we might have, and in many ways shifts our cognitions about ourselves and increases our confidence about engaging in the world.

That concept of the therapeutic alliance applies to most professions, not just psychotherapy. I say to clients, "If you've got a physician that you don't like, and you don't trust, and they just simply tell you to take a medication, are you more or less likely to be treatment compliant than if that physician were kind, had a good bedside manner, took time to understand who you were, and explained the rationale for why that treatment would be helpful?" Most people say, "Well, definitely I'd be more treatment compliant if I trusted my physician."

The power of trust to create positive change applies across the board to almost any profession and relationship. In situations where our biases and negative or inaccurate assumptions about people become apparent, trust is lost, and the therapeutic relationship is put in danger.

Assumptions tied to racism, xenophobia, and a lack of cultural competence have a greater disruption on trust, because they reflect systemic societal racism. These biases that come to the surface without our awareness can relay a failure of egalitarianism, but also a lack of compassion and insight. The entire relationship and trust are at risk when we are complacent about not identifying our assumptions, because trust, in the context of ongoing societal injustices, is a very fragile thing.

Many of us have known people we have trusted for the longest time and then find that they engage in behavior that makes us realize that perhaps we have not understood them, or they have not truly understood us. All of a sudden trust is gone. Trust is being constantly reevaluated. Trust is being constantly built, and there needs to be mindfulness for that trust. When we remove a better sense of understanding, when there is not a sense of egalitarianism, or when there is a demonstration of a power imbalance, then I think trust is violated.

Awareness and implementation of social justice build trust and egalitarianism

Trust is about justice. Though some professions, such as those in health, require information to be collected up front (e.g., an intake evaluation), the ability to be the author of one's own story, instead of having a story, or stereotype, thrust upon a client, is necessary for trust and justice. It is important to remember that outside of this working relationship, people of color experience ongoing racism, microaggressions, and marginalization, where stereotypical stories are thrust upon the clients with whom we work. If we continue to do the same, the working relationship and trust becomes no different from the experiences of marginalization our clients face in the everyday world. Justice and trust are about being heard, and sustaining control over your own experience.

A culmination of the points discussed thus far for effective cross-cultural competence, includes the following:

1. The best work that a therapist or any professional can do to be culturally competent is to investigate their own biases and worldviews.
   Working cross-culturally in a socially just way means recognition that the work being done is not just about the client, but the practitioner too. Though the practitioner comes to the table with their own expertise, the expectation that they are an expert in the cultural experience of the client is incorrect. Even in a helpful working relationship, the work being done is as much about the helper as it is about the client.

2. It is important that biases and assumptions are identified and discussed up front. That means if a practitioner has a misunderstanding, rather than ignore it and have it influence therapy, the practitioner must be honest with themselves to acknowledge the misunderstanding. In some or most cases, these issues must be discussed before they can be clarified. This demonstrates a willingness not only to understand but to address a better understanding of the person with whom you are working, and the relevant issues they present. This can be done by confirming that a practitioner does not have the cultural knowledge or awareness about the experience of the client, and wants to ensure they proceed with accurate information, and that the door to correcting misinformation remains open with the client.

3. Though you do not need to assume things about the client, being aware of common cultural issues over the course of time can help you understand and appreciate your client. Initial impressions can be fine-tuned through discussion, and corrected if necessary. Remember that although

the practitioner can ask the client to keep them informed about relevant information tied to the situation specific to why they are seeking help, that work to obtain this information can also be done on the practitioner's own time, working outside the working relationship. This can be time consuming, but it is essential. You do not want to use the client to educate yourself, instead of using your time together to meet their needs.

In short, there are two crucial elements: one's personal awareness and one's skill as a therapist. Remember also that becoming culturally competent will take time. We work first with the information we have until we are better informed to act better. As Maya Angelou taught us, do your best until you know better. And when you know better, do better.

3

Bias

3.1   The Perspective of the Therapist

The following chapters will break down critical issues, loosely related to the Collins and Arthur model for culturally sensitive therapy. This next section will focus on the work required to be done by the practitioner in better understanding their own perspectives, biases, and how they impact a cross-cultural working alliance.

3.2   Bias Defined

According to Merriam-Webster (n.d., Bias), bias is "an inclination of temperament or outline, a personal and sometimes unreasoned judgement, and a prejudice." But the definition of bias is less important, than the reasons we might carry it, and what it produces. And even more importantly, the perception of what it means to carry bias and the toll of seeing this bias to the admission and discussion of it, can lead to more equitable relationships with people. The term "bias" is fraught with tension and anxiety, and associated, as noted in the definition by Merriam-Webster, with prejudice, or in some cases, assumed discrimination or racism.

We obtain bias through our life experiences. This includes all forms of socialization and learning, including exposure to beliefs and worldviews in education, work, and the media. According to Gerbner (1998) and classic *cultivation theory*, our worldview changes based on what we see around us. Since there is a White standard in the world with a history of colonialism (Gray, 2019; Okun et al., 2019) it makes sense that our bias leans toward seeing the White world as the measuring stick by which we measure all others. The data from a recent bias tool I developed, titled *Bias Outside the Box* (the BOB tool; see Appendix 1; https://leadwithdiversity.com/testbias/), as reported in Abdulrehman and Clara (2023) show that bias toward White supremacy (seeing White people as local and people of color as foreign, having greater empathy and relatability toward White people than people of color, seeing people of color as non-English speakers, etc.) shows that a large percentage of the population tend to carry such biases, including people of color, immigrants, and both men and women.

According to other research (Gran-Ruaz et al., 2022; Ramasubramanian, 2010), false stereotypes and a lack of representation in the media and the world around us cause people to internalize stereotypes and stratify Whiteness above all others; this occurs with people of color and those from nondominant cultures. Furthermore, the lack of inclusive messages in our world causes White people and those from dominant cultures to have an artificially enhanced sense of self-worth as a culture and an ethnicity. And so, this inclination toward Whiteness (the measuring stick) can often become the means by which we see those of us we perceive to be different from us. But also, even as people of color or those from a nondominant culture, we also carry these biases (Abdulrehman & Clara, 2023; M. T. Williams et al., 2021), this internalized policing (racism) can also cause people of color to use Whiteness as the measuring stick for what they consider normal. This causes Whiteness to be centered in our engagement with others, and this most certainly shows up in the therapy room or any other professional relationship, given that our beliefs and thoughts impact not just our emotions about people, but how we engage with them. When we are not mindful of the beliefs, or biases we hold, our emotions remain unchecked, as does our behavior toward others, making cross-cultural competence difficult. Reviewing our own bias means questioning the way we see others and the world, and also commonly established practices and institutions, as systemic racism is fairly common.

We must be thoughtful of how our society and we ourselves are White centered

The implications of a White-centered bias can be damaging to any effort to a culturally sensitive working alliance, including in therapy, if the practitioner remains blind to the biases they hold personally, but also the presence of White supremacy in our current world and society. Regardless of profession, we tend to approach a working relationship, focusing on the target problem without necessarily paying attention to the systems that contribute to the problem. In therapy, we might focus on mental health issues, or the more direct social circumstances that influence mental health. In other professions we could focus on physical health, finances, education – but we always focus on solitary elements of the individual. When we see these elements of our relationship as isolated, without understanding they are strongly influenced by a larger societal standard of White supremacy, we are then blind to them, and are likely to promote those biases in the working relationship with our client.

According to Sue (2019), each community of individuals still has general themes of beliefs associated with that group. For example, Sue notes that Black people are generally associated with danger and criminal behavior, and gay people with sinfulness. These may not be your beliefs, but research confirms that these biases still exist in modern day society, and that many of us do actually hold biases about different people that are stereotypical (Abdulrehman & Clara, 2023). Some of these stereotypes have shown up with the BOB tool, where common beliefs include that Arab men are more likely to challenge what people perceive as "Western" beliefs, that Black men are not likely to be professionals, and that South Asian women are less likely to have English as a first language.

3.3　Your Own Worldview and Bias

We become anxious when addressing our biases (Kanter et al., 2019), and we can experience significant distress because of the fear of being labeled racist. Yet, ironically, not addressing our biases increases our blind spots, and the chances we may inadvertently carry out racist or discriminatory behaviors that alienate our clients and destroy trust. One of the other challenges with bias is that we often do not have a mirror held up to ourselves, and so there are limited opportunities to acknowledge and change our behavior. The BOB tool was developed with this in mind, allowing individuals to respond to a variety of visual images of diverse people in a variety of cultural clothing, needing to respond to a series of questions. It allows for individuals to begin to have an honest conversation with themselves, with the rationale for their decisions being questioned in the end. Though there are clear-cut correct responses, they are not revealed in this tool, as the purpose is not about being right or wrong, but rather about using the BOB tool to explore the rationale for the immediate "gut reaction" choices we make, as those most clearly reveal and reflect our biases.

Many people believe they are not biased, because they are fundamentally opposed to largely historical and more exaggerated examples of racism. Many people consider the concept of racism and discrimination to be tied to Apartheid, separate seating spaces, and lynches and hangings. What people do not consider is what racism looks and feels like today, from the experience of people of color, and of those from nondominant cultural communities, and as such they remain blind to these realities.

Before we review the findings of the BOB tool, it is helpful to first review what racism looks like today, as when working with cross-cultural clientele, the likelihood of them being people of color or from marginalized cultural communities, is high. Being aware of the propensity toward discrimination these clients experience, and how you the practitioner may perpetuate this discrimination, is critically important for cross-cultural work.

3.4　Definition of Racism

Racism and discrimination are not only about what is done actively, but also about what is done passively. Racism and discrimination are so entrenched in our cultural system that we center being White ethnically and culturally. White people are more commonly and positively presented in media, White people are more likely to be hired for higher paying and leadership roles, and though we may not agree to violence against people of color, that dominance and presence of one ethnicity and culture over others becomes internalized by people living in this society, including people who are marginalized. And in the same way that Clark and Clark (1947) found that children of color in the late 1940s and early 1950s preferred to play with, and attributed more positive qualities toward, White dolls than dolls that were Black, current research has confirmed similar findings (Parsons et al., 2019). In the Western world, when we think of leadership, we think White (Gundemir et al., 2014). Not only do we prefer White leaders, but we tend to assign more positive qualities to White leaders than leaders of color. And so just because there are leaders of color present in our society does not erase the vestiges of racism in our minds, whether we label ourselves as racists or not. Racism, bias, xenophobia, and other forms of discrimination can show up in our interactions with others, and these psychological concepts are still alive and well. Although the burning crosses that represented White supremacy (and the terror of racism that came with them) may not be as frequent as they were in our recent past, those burning crosses remain well-lit and burning in our minds and in our systems of practice, regardless of our intention or awareness.

Whiteness is about culture as well as ethnicity. The norms and expectations by which we live our lives are based on White or Eurocentric culture, including what we celebrate (e.g., focusing on Christmas with a White Santa as dominant vs. any other cultural or religious holiday), names, an expectation of what constitutes healthy family relationships and attachment, what information we expect people to share with us, and clothing. All of this is centered on what we have been used to, or learned to tolerate, in a social structure that was created when people of color were openly subjugated, and Canada and the US were (and still are) ruled by White people and their beliefs. In order for people of color, or those from nondominant cultural communities, to have upward mobility, they have needed to, and still do need to, acculturate to White-centric culture. Those who have difficulties acculturating are deemed problematic, and those who are able to are seen as model minorities (Ching, 2022; Panelo, 2010; Shukla et al., 2020). As such, Whiteness and its supremacy is also promoted by people of color as well; in some cases, people of color police themselves to fit in or be accepted by a White dominant culture. This phenomenon is so prevalent, that communities of color have developed language to point out the need to switch behavior to match a White cultural standard. The term "code switching," now defined in the Oxford Dictionary as "alternating between two or more languages, or varieties of languages in a conversation," is colloquially used to describe the switching of social behaviors and norms of people of color and those from nondominant cultural communities to fit in with the White world, particularly the professional world. The need to be able to code switch for survival is so strong in fact, that some people have simply given up their culture, and adopted a "White way" of living as a permanent code switch. This can then be inherited by multiple generations, in the same way that my grandfather, father, and now I, have adopted what was British dress as what the quintessential "well-dressed man" wears, as the measuring stick for appropriate garb, ultimately erasing culture and perspectives from families and ultimately society. But the ability to be a model minority and code switch to sustain success in a White world is often at odds with the importance of sustaining culture in many people of color. This impacts ethnic and cultural identity development (reviewed later in Chapter 4 but also throughout this book). But cultural sterilizing has led to the development of terms across a variety of cultural communities of color in Canada, the US, and many parts of the Western World such as the UK and Australia, that describes people who have given up their cultural perspectives. It is a profound realization that regardless of what term is used, all reflect the White wash and sterilization of culture, as a result of internalized racism in a broad range of communities of color, all of which have been the victims of White supremacy. Words such as "coconut," "Twinkie," "banana," "Oreo," "double-stuffed Oreo" (referring to being extra White inside), and "apple" all refer to having cultural perspectives removed, and being colored on the outside but White on the inside and are used in pejorative ways. This is the strength of racism today. And if people of color can be impacted, knowing, seeing, and experiencing racism, it can be taken as a surety that when those with White privilege are blind to it, that they have internalized White supremacy without recognizing it. And so many will engage in racist behaviors that marginalize and discriminate, without realizing it, only because they are sustaining the norms of what they know (be it beauty, cultural expectations, professional behavior, etc.). Being unaware of their own White supremacy increases their chances of removing any sense of cultural sensitivity. In this way, racism is not always about what is done, but what is not done, what we are complacent about, and allow to occur, continuously placing those who are not White and those from nondominant cultures and their experiences second. In this way, racism today is primarily psychological, and internalized in both White people and people of color. Without challenging this in every fiber of our engagement with ourselves and others, the former generations of colonialists and conscious White supremacists will have been successful in sustaining a stratification of ethnicity and culture as the standard in not just Canada, the US, and many western countries, but globally.

3.5   Ignorance and Bias

Though we may use softer terms such as "ignorance" or "bias," what we must realize is that all of these come from racism and result in racism if not checked, whether we realize it or not. Being unaware of the marginalization we may be furthering with our clients makes the impact of that insensitivity more harmful, and infuses racism into the nature of the relationship, promoting an unspoken power dynamic. For this reason, acknowledging the differences, the lack of awareness, and inherent White supremacy is necessary in cross-cultural work. Receptivity from marginalized individuals may vary dependent on their own ethnic and cultural identity development (how much of a "coconut" they may be), which will be explored in Chapter 4. But acknowledging the power differential of Whiteness in the world, and saying to your client that you yourself are still learning, talking about those issues that are relevant, when needed, and you remain open to them, can go a long way in establishing trust. Without this, any bias or ignorance may layer upon the heaps of both small and large experiences of discrimination your client

Softer terminology doesn't reduce the impact of racism

may have faced. Acknowledging it, regardless of whether they have normalized the experience of racism or not, allows them to understand they no longer need to normalize it with you.

3.6   Bias in Canada and the US

As noted above, it is often believed that because many of us are philosophically against the concept of racism or discrimination, then we do not engage in it ourselves, or at the very least, it becomes difficult to accept that we carry bias that can then lead to behaviors that are racist and discriminatory. We may also feel that because we have faced hardship that we are immune to the concepts of privilege, in particular White privilege. Yet the concept of privilege from a social justice perspective is systemic, and ideologies of preference are sustained societally. Furthermore, it might be easier to believe the stereotypes that those who hold the most bias or at greater risk for having views that promote racism are those with the most privilege: White men. None of that, according to data from a review of responses to the BOB tool, is true (Abdulrehman & Clara, 2023).

Reviewing the biases shown by predominantly Canadians and Americans (Abdulrehman & Clara, 2023), ($N = 5,065$), we found that generally speaking, people (gender and ethnicity not accounted for) carried biases of xenophobia toward people who were not White and who dressed in clothing that was not perceived as "Western," including seeing them to be more likely to be foreign born, more likely to not speak English or have it as their second language, more likely to have views that challenged "Western values," less likely to have the privileges of wealth, and less likely to be professionals. The initial analyses also found that White people were more likely to have greater empathy or compassion for other White people, that Black women were perceived to be less likely than White women or other women of color to be the victim of abuse by men, and that White people and other people of color were more likely to be seen as successful compared with Indigenous people.

Though BIPOC people were less likely to have these biases, they still carried them. What was also interesting is that in some circumstances, White women were more likely to hold biases against people of color than were White men (Faber & Lei, 2023). In both of these cases, individuals were expected to have less bias, due to being marginalized, still carried bias, and in some cases more than those with greater privilege (Abdulrehman & Clara, 2023). What this also says is that when working to address bias, we cannot assume that because we have experienced some marginalization, it frees us from the necessity to explore our own perspectives, worldviews, and potential biases. Examples of colorism in communities of color suggest that at many times, people of color or those from nondominant cultural communities can show racism toward their own community or other communities of color. Bias, and the impacts of it, including racism, are complex social phenomena that are psychological in nature and impact all of us, with the understanding that experiencing marginalization and being aware of its impact creates some protection against committing racism (M. T. Williams & Sharif, 2021).

In other biases examined on the BOB tool, besides the ones discussed above, we found only minor differences between White men and White women. This suggests *that actually the level of privilege and bias was almost as high and some cases higher in White women than it was in White men.* There was a high level of xenophobia found in these responses of people across respondents from Canada and the US predominantly, which is a common bias. I think many people of color, regardless of where they were born, even if they were Indigenous, often talk about their experiences of feeling like an outsider. What we actually find in this data is that it is true that people of color, including Indigenous people who are not foreigners, are still seen as foreigners. They are less likely to be seen as individuals who speak English, less likely to be seen as having economic privilege, and less likely to be seen as being successful. The exception noted to the last perception on success was only when a South Asian woman was wearing nontraditional clothing and more likely to be perceived as a medical specialist, confirming the commonly held belief that some people of color are good immigrants by casting aside their culture to adopt White culture, and become professionals.

So, whereas White immigrants tended to be seen to be more likely local people, more likely to be speaking English, and more likely to have European ancestry, whereas people of color, even those who did have some European ancestry, were not seen in any way as having some European ancestry. There is a great level of xenophobia present in these data, even though a large percentage of the population studied were White female, center to left leaning, and highly educated. The other thing we found was that regardless of the level of education, highly educated people were just as biased as the less educated.

People who responded to the BOB tool (which was publicized through a variety of methods including social media, corporate sponsorship, an art show, and word of mouth through other DEI trainers) tended to internalize and have views of White supremacy across the board. Differences in levels of bias occurred when people had diverse experiences. For example, in some situations, we found transgender respondents to carry less bias than cis-gendered people. In other situations, there was no difference between trans and cisgendered people. The same was true for BIPOC people and immigrants, depending on the question; for some questions, BIPOC individuals were less likely than White people to show any bias.

The experience of being different allows us to reduce the bias that we carry in certain areas, and it provides us with empathy and clear relatability. This was particularly fascinating, even among transgender people who are White, as the ability to create relatability was not tied to ethnicity in this situation. Having the experience of being marginalized allowed greater clarity in how we see people who are perceived as different. As the saying goes, misery loves company; a more accurate interpretation is that understanding the challenges of others produces greater empathy and the ability to understand a different cultural experience.

3.7   Examples

3.7.1   Example One

One such example of being marginalized occurred with a colleague of mine, Soo Kim, who is Canadian, but who immigrated from Korea when she was young. Though she and I had both immigrated from two completely different geographic and cultural regions of the world, in a few brief but relatable and thus intimate conversations, she described feeling as though she and I were "kin." And in a discussion on my podcast, *Different People* (Abdulrehman, 2021), we discussed the common experience of immigration, feeling like an outsider, both growing up in families that made their living running a small grocery store, and experiencing similar levels of challenges with racism and White supremacy in the professional world. Though we shared common elements in both of our cultural histories, the ability to relate to our post immigration experiences was far more powerful in connecting and feeling safe with each other to the point of feeling kinship. Had she and I been White, or not had experiences we could relate to, or had unchecked biases, our ability to relate cross-culturally would have been greatly diminished. And in the podcast episode, we also discussed the fact that the ability to be vulnerable with individuals who did not understand or express an understanding of our post-immigration experiences (i.e., White friends and colleagues) was far diminished. When they understood our experiences, our ability to feel closer and more open to those people we considered friends and colleagues was far greater.

3.7.2   Example Two

Paul was one of the kindest individuals you could met. He was well known, well published, and known to many as "Saint Paul." He made every effort to lift up those who needed assistance and create opportunities for new colleagues. He had no malice, and he would be the last person anyone would consider a racist.

One day, Paul asked a colleague to take over a client, a young Filipino teenage girl. Paul was sensitive to the issue of age difference, and he thought a younger psychologist would relate more to her and be a better age fit. The client's primary difficulties were social anxiety, but because Paul did not have the experience of being an immigrant, as both the client and the younger colleague had, he had a blind spot regarding a critical element that contributed to her social anxiety; she was excessively shy about being around her parents who spoke little English, and she was working hard to come across as an assimilated Canadian.

Though Paul had no negative views about this young girl, her family, or her community, his lack of relatability to her cultural experiences prevented him from being able to address a critical concern. The primary barrier (which he originally perceived as age) was in fact one of cultural experience. Had

Paul considered this, and done the work to understand the experience, some direct discussion about those experiences, and his expression of the understanding of that experience, would have facilitated his work with her.

The example above points out how the lack of awareness of what we are missing – simplifying issues tied to age, in this example, versus culture – creates a blind spot that can interfere with a practitioner providing service. In this example, it was something missed, rather than something done to create disparity between a practitioner and a client. In both cases, they can be equally damaging. Missing a critical issue can have a paramount impact on therapeutic outcomes.

Sometimes, the absence of a question relays a worldview of the practitioner or their openness to discussing the issue, which influences not just the conceptualization of a patient's situation, but also any treatment advice offered.

When it comes to culture, ethnicity, and race, why are experiences of people of color or those from nondominant cultures not relatable to people who do not belong to those groups (White people)? In contrast, the experiences common to White people are relatable to all people. Consider Christmas. Regardless of culture, geography, or ethnicity, everyone is aware of Christmas and the nuances tied to that cultural celebration (of a predominantly White Eurocentric culture). Even as you read this, there will be people who will rebut this with "but Christmas is common everywhere!" It is not, but it appears so due to the adoption of White and Eurocentric culture. Interestingly, we are not as familiar with the nuances and celebrations of Hindu, Jewish, or Muslim communities, despite those global communities being sizeable. Again, this points toward a cultural preference for White supremacy, and all complacent White individuals are partially responsible for this (see Appendix 2).

3.7.3   Example Three

Here is a powerful example of how the worldview of what and who is local versus foreign influences trust and the ability to build more inclusive working environments in a situation where the intention may not have been so positive. A child was attending a preschool that had a very diverse group of students. The child's parent noted to the director of the school that they did a beautiful job honoring and celebrating Christmas, and with the diverse student body they could perhaps also work to celebrate the holidays of the other students with the same level of enthusiasm as the students showed for Christmas.

The focus on Christmas or Christian-based holidays in our society speaks to White supremacy

The director responded that they already learned about international communities, and that was enough, refusing to do more. The parent persisted and reminded the director that the students in the class were not international, but local, and their holidays should be celebrated as local traditions.

The director became defensive and claimed to understand but refused to do any such thing. They said they understood that this was important to immigrants, because the director had worked with people from a particular school (in a less affluent community), and so they understood why this was important to the parent but still did not feel it was a relevant issue in this school's neighborhood. The parent reminded the director that their family did not live in the less affluent part of the city, and that they lived in the catchment of the current school on the opposite end of the city, as did the families of many of the diverse students there. Despite having this pointed out to them, the director was reluctant to make any changes or acknowledge their biased (and some would say racist) beliefs. Here was an example where a refusal to admit blindness and misinformation caused not only a lack of trust but created a sense of marginalization and psychological trauma to me, the families, and the students of that school, who were taught the celebration of one community, the community of the director of the school, was more important than anyone else's celebration.

3.7.4   Example Four

There are numerous biases about people from different cultural and religious groups. One child I knew was a boy whose parents were Muslim, and they had been going through a separation. The boy reported that he was being abused by his mother. There were clear signs of abuse, the boy manifested symptoms of trauma, had bruising indicative of abuse, and there were numerous concerned parties who contacted child and family services to make reports. Despite the mounting evidence of abuse, it was continuously ignored for years. The mother, a Muslim woman, claimed that she was emancipating herself from an abusive husband who was a "practicing Muslim." There was no evidence of domestic abuse by the husband, despite investigation, but the claim was made anyway. The child and family services worker took these statements as facts because they fit a sad but common stereotype reflected in Western culture. The bias (believing that Muslim women are victims and Muslim men are abusers) resulted in the evidence presented by the child and numerous professionals concerned about abuse being completely ignored. In this case, an unfounded assumption, a stereotype, and a desire to help the mother (who was a Muslim woman who needed to be saved from a Muslim man) influenced the safety and well-being of a young boy (Illustrations 2a–2d).

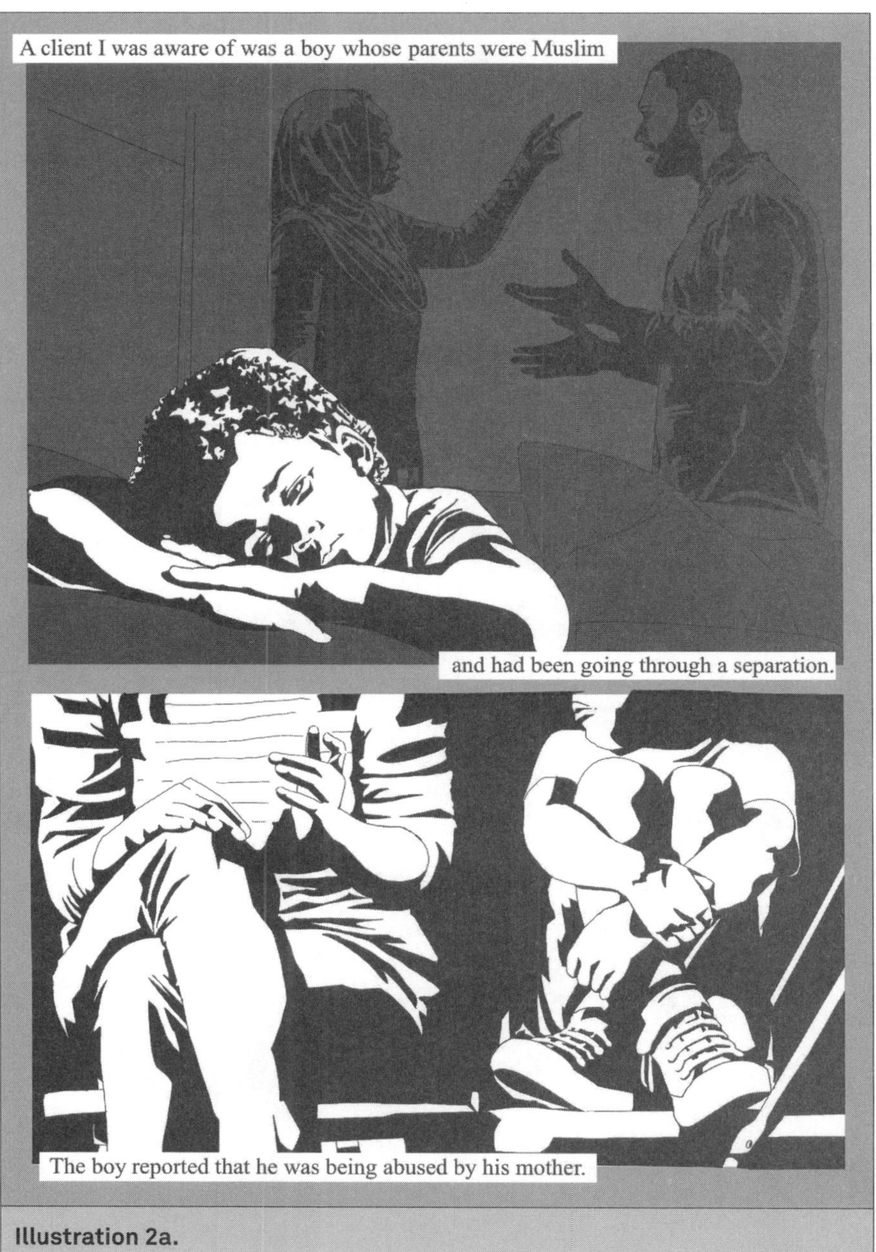

Illustration 2a.

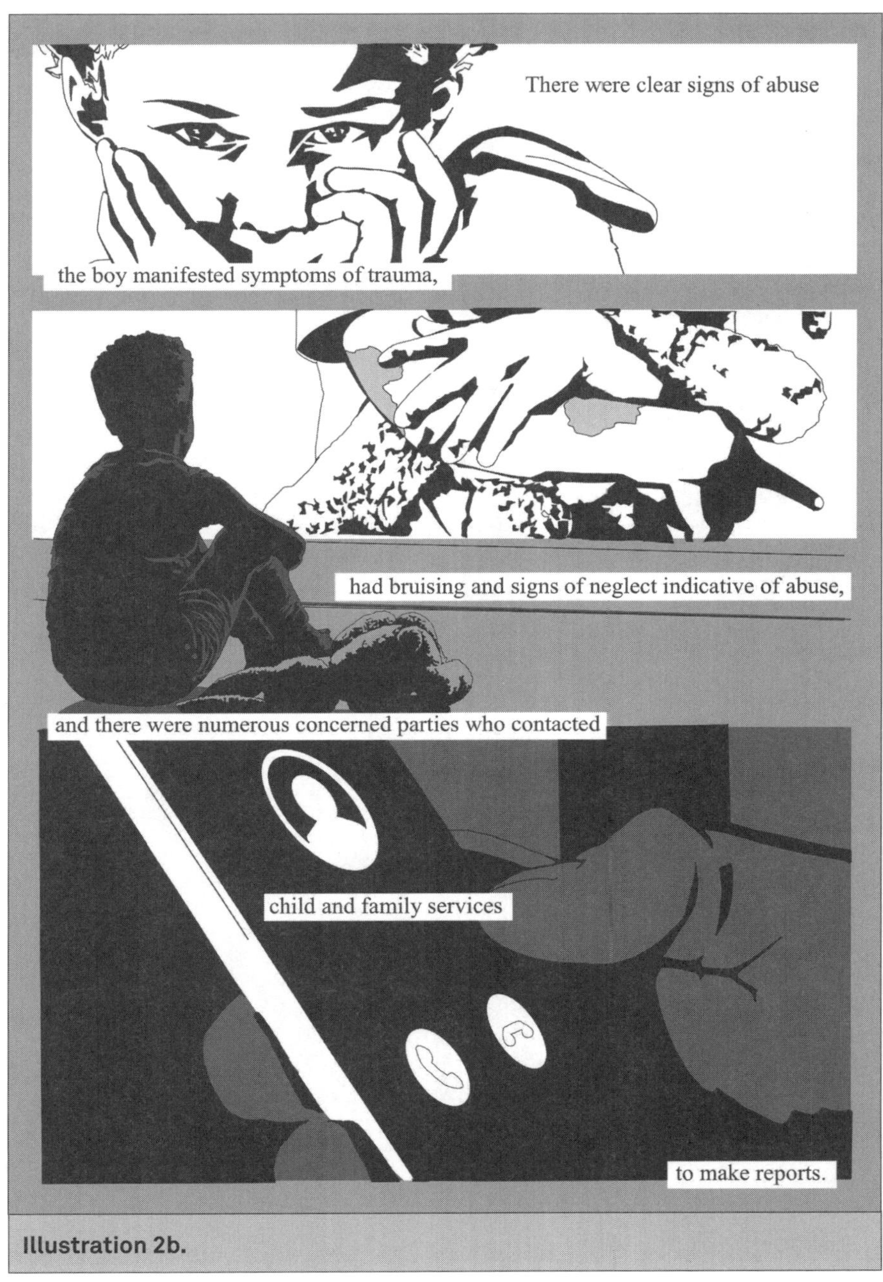

Illustration 2b.

Illustration 2c.

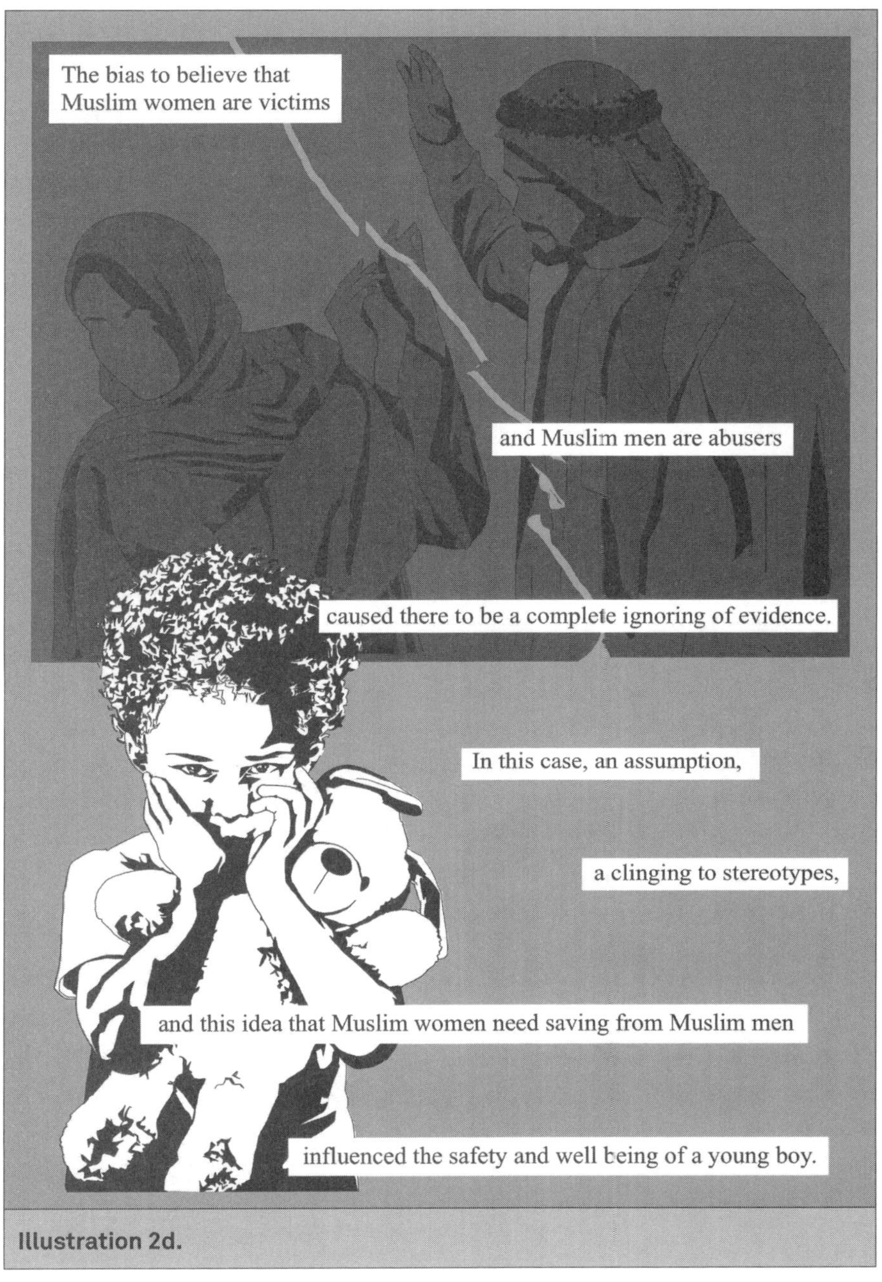

Illustration 2d.

3.7.5 Example Five

Cultural Ethnicity and Rewarding Assimilation (Because of Assumptions)

A young girl is a refugee from a Middle Eastern country and goes to see a therapist and says that she's struggling with her identity and her culture and talks about being embarrassed about being around her father. She's a practicing Muslim, and would take off her headscarf at school and would have to put it back on when she came back home. The message often given to this person by educators and health professionals was one that would seem to be a supportive one: that you can be who you need to be. Nobody should force a religion on you or a way of life, and good for you for taking off your headscarf. She was told she should stand up to her family and tell them what she "actually believed."

This kind of message of support, without recognizing many issues tied to cultural supremacy and ethnic and cultural identity development issues in many immigrant children, proselytizes a dominant culture. There was no assessment, no space left for the conceptualization. The reason she had difficulty was not because she had a problem with her beliefs, but rather because she was made to feel like an outsider by everybody at school. And she had articulated that on numerous occasions. She said that was not the problem. "It's just, I never felt like I belonged, and people judged me a lot." Actually, when she took off her headscarf, because she's fair-skinned and has blonde hair and light-colored eyes, she passed as White and was rewarded by people not identifying her as a person of color, and she experienced less racism and marginalization as a result; rewarding Whiteness.

There was a lot more reward in it. In this case, there was an assumption similar to those that health professionals make about men and boys and victims, based on a worldview that influenced how they asked, what they asked, and, in this case, any discussion of assimilation, or encouragement to, assimilate.

The examples above speak to powerful microaggressions that have macro impacts, as also noted by Sue & Spanierman (2020). It is important also to understand that microaggressions are really the behavioral outcome of what we think and feel. Being unaware of how we see the world, and any inaccuracies in that, will perpetuate problematic behavior and emotions. More specifically, we now understand the power of a thought, and how disregarding or being complacent about the biases we carry are dangerous to people of color. The last two examples above specifically point to how biases can have frighteningly negative impacts on the physical and psychological health of children of color, without the slightest hint of concern or awareness in the people who do the damage.

3.7.6 Anxiety About Bias

Reading the above examples may make some people feel that relatability is impossible. And many others fear that by identifying their own biases, they risk being labeled as racists, claiming their actions were not intentional. It is important, however, to understand that intent is different from outcome. And regardless of intention, regardless of language used to describe the problem, having a society built upon White supremacy makes racism that inhibits cultural competence a probable outcome for many. Though challenging and uncomfortable, like any anxiety, the more open we become to talking about the internalized beliefs we hold, the greater comfort we have in those discussions and the greater ability we obtain in challenging internalized biases and racist outcomes. It is, though difficult, the only way to begin. At times, this can be done with personal tools (e.g., the BOB tool), and at other times, it requires ongoing conversations with colleagues and friends. In other situations, having a coach or a consultant (ideally a psychologist) who does this work is necessary to address our own biases. Overcoming our biases is a cultural problem that exists in many Western countries for many people.

3.7.7   What Happens When We Are Not Mindful of Bias

In other situations, the lack of awareness of information missed, or of biases, can be more direct, and it can openly threaten trust and safety.

According to Derald Wing Sue (2019), microaggressions are everyday verbal, nonverbal, or environmental slights, snubs, or insults, whether they are intentional or unintentional, which communicate hostile, derogatory, or negative messages to target a person based solely upon their marginalized group membership. These hidden messages may invalidate the group identity or the experiential reality of target persons, demean them on a personal or a group level, communicate that they are lesser human beings, suggest they do not belong with the majority group, threaten and intimidate, and relegate them to inferior status or treatment.

3.8   Solutions

> **1. Be open to your biases and admit an error when it occurs. Talk openly about it with yourself and your clients.**

Talk openly about biases, instead of passively waiting for it to be brought up by your client. To bring it up, say, *"Let me know if I have, at any point, said something wrong, because I'm in the process of learning, and in the process of improving my cultural competence."* What that does is make space to have those discussions as therapy progresses. It prevents defensiveness, and it opens the doors for a heartier discussion. And, further, one might say, *"I'm working on that. I'm going to acknowledge that right off the top. I recognize that not everything is about ethnicity or culture or race. I also recognize that I'm not a person of color / a person from your background. I'm working on this path, and*

I'm not going to be colorblind. I am going to acknowledge that there are differences in people and differences in experiences, and I'm going to recognize there are similarities. I would appreciate it if you would let me know in my work if I've missed any mark, and I'll be open to that." Imagine the kind of reaction you would get when you said that.

I think you would get one of two reactions, depending on where your client is at in their own cultural and ethnic identity development: "Why is that the important thing here? I came to see you as a professional. Why is my ethnicity the first thing you're going to see?" or "I appreciate your acknowledging that."

Regardless of which response you get, you will have addressed a topic that needs to be addressed. Remember also that as a professional, you are meant to raise uncomfortable topics, particularly in the case of health and mental health. It does not mean that you need to discuss that uncomfortable topic, but addressing it can open the door for a better conversation when it arises later. In the case of cross-cultural issues, you will have taken the unspoken and given it space, being as clear as you possibly can, and you will have indicated that you are willing to address issues of race, ethnicity, and culture.

If the reaction is negative, you can say, *"Look, I can choose to be somebody who pretends to be colorblind, or I can be somebody who chooses to acknowledge the impact that racism and discrimination have on people and the role they can play in any part of life. I'm going to be honest and open to that. That means sometimes I recognize what I've done wrong. I can choose to be open, or I can choose to be closed, and it may have come across as offensive, but it is my intention to try to make sure that it's not ignored. I want to make sure if it may not have anything to do with what we're going to talk about. I would like you to know that this is a place that you can point out errors that I make."*

Even the negative response opens the door to talking about what you want to do. We do not necessarily need to be confident about our abilities or the lack of bias, but confident in our ability and willingness to learn and acknowledge error and mistake. That is the piece we need to be the most confident about.

> **2. Do not try to be colorblind. Doing so removes the differences in experience, including racism and xenophobia, that are necessary and valid parts of the experience of your client.**

Sometimes when somebody is not comfortable with their ethnic and cultural identity, it is useful to help them identify their discomfort. Sometimes the negative responses that we get or the failure to acknowledge cultural differences are due to a lack of comfort in our own cultural and ethnic identity. The need to be White and not recognized as a person of color can create a defensiveness. People who are comfortable with their ethnic and cultural identity development are not going to have an issue being identified as having a different experience, because they know what their experience is. What I say to people generally, when they come in to see me is *"I might be an expert in mental health, but I'm not an expert in your life experience. I will understand and see things from the perspective of my training. I will know what I'm looking for in a diagnosis (or the professional opinion you are seeking), but I want to understand what your experiences are like, and it will be up to you to inform me about what that experience is like, because I need to know that to work with you."*

For example, I do not drink alcohol, as it is not been a part of my culture in any way. A lot of people use references to alcohol when I work with them describing how much they have drunk (e.g., a Mickey, a two-four). Being unaware of these measurements – or even the type of alcohol being discussed – I have had to ask clients to inform me, but also to do my own research, and make note of the cultural differences. This allows me to then get clarity about how much my client drinks. It took a lot of learning on my part to understand what alcohol consumption was, because almost all of the people I worked with drank alcohol, and I did not, and all of their references to alcohol consumption were over my head. If I had not taken the time to understand it, and to learn on my own, I would have been missing out on a critical assessment component of my work with clients.

Similarly, when I work with people from the lesbian, gay, bisexual, transgender, queer/questioning, and asexual (LGBTQ+) community, I say to them, *"I need to understand certain aspects about your life. If I've said something wrong, you're going to have to let me know that I've said something wrong."* When I work with people who are transgender, I say, *"My intention is to make sure that I get your pronouns correctly. If I miss them, correct me and know that my intention is in the right place."* This does not mean it is okay to say the wrong thing. It is okay for the patient to correct me, because that will help me get it. I might say, *"It is empowering to anybody who does not have it: I will speak to my expertise. You help me understand your experience from that. Now I will present to you what I understand. If I don't get it, I need you to tell me."*

When we do cross-cultural work, we just need to be up front and say, *"Look, there might be a difference of experience. If there is, I need you to let me know. I'm not making the assumption based on your ethnicity, but I do recognize I'm not colorblind. I recognize there is a difference in our names. There might be a difference in our culture and our experiences. I want to put that on the table. When, and if it comes up, I've put it here. I'm not going to pretend like I don't have biases. But I am going to ensure I work hard and change the ones that I may have inherited. I'm going to put it on the table and working through these issues will become part of our work. I will do my own education as well, but sometimes you'll need to guide me on your experience."*

Put simply, you admit to yourself, as well as to this other person, that you're growing. *"Psychotherapy is a journey in growth. I appreciate you educating me; I know that was not your primary purpose, but it's happening."*

Statements such as these diffuse some of the disparity. We talked earlier about White supremacy and how White supremacy is almost always dominant. When somebody comes into a one-on-one session, the unwritten script is that there is a disparity between Whiteness and people of color. If you have privilege that you are blind to, you will not recognize this power differential. When you acknowledge it, you create a sense of justice and remove yourself from the cultural driver's seat.

Decentering Whiteness, and in the case of a White practitioner, decentering their cultural perspective to center the client's cultural perspective, is the ultimate example of client-centered practice.

3. Reframe your definition of who is in your community and learn more about the people in your community.

If a member of your family told you they were vegan, you would naturally make an effort to learn about their dietary restrictions and ensure meals in the household were made to ensure nutritional needs were met and the meals were tasty. If a member of your family told you they were gay, you would make efforts to accept them, even if you might not have grown up in a context that accepted same-sex relationships. But because you consider them a part of your family, a part of your community, the effort to learn and understand their perspective becomes paramount to their inclusion and your ability to learn to ensure they are not rejected by things you say or do not say, to ensure trust is maintained and even built upon further. That is not always the case in how we approach people in our community who come from different ethnic and cultural groups. To become culturally competent, one must first begin to accept people who are different from you as a part of your own community and work toward their inclusion. Our definition of community needs to change. We must accept that local communities, including our own, are more diverse than we realize.

We need to move forward in a way that we understand the differences in people as a part of understanding our communities. I am not White, but White people live in my community so I must understand them. It is important for me to understand what my community is in the same way that a Jew, a Muslim, a Black man, or a gay Asian woman is a part of a larger community, and they consider themselves a part of that larger community. White people need to understand the experiences of people other than their own too, because they are a part of that larger community too.

Actually, if people do not move toward cultural competence, we cannot consider ourselves to live and operate in a modern society. We can no longer afford for cross-cultural competence to be an optional skill, and it must be taught in every professional school. Not doing this is unprofessional and unethical.

There is a difference between our personal and professional identities, but the two identities draw from each other. The questions we need to be asking are, what have we done to increase our experiences personally? Do we have friends from different groups? Do we go to different places? Do we persist in activities and engagement that retain only a single perspective, and keep our world small? We may, for example, keep our sense of community very circumscribed, culturally and ethnically. Going to cultural events of other communities, we see ourselves as learning about others. In actual fact, we are also learning about ourselves.

The implicit bias here is that *my* community is a White community. It is not spoken, but it does exist. This bias can also exist within communities of color, depending on the person. We will see *their* communities as being different, and not see *their* community as a part of ours. This is where *code switching* occurs: I need to be myself. I can only be myself in a community that will accept me. I cannot be myself in a larger White community. I must act White to belong to a dominant culture. Anybody reading this book who comes from a White background or a dominant culture needs to ask themselves, am I inclusive in my community, in my definition of community, and in my engagement with community (Illustration 3)?

Illustration 3.

Let's imagine someone wants to learn about Asian people as a part of their community. If this is done in an overly aggressive way, in a way that is not sensitive to the differences, it will be perceived as patronizing. For example, if one just went to eat at an Asian restaurant once or a few times to learn about the culture of a broader community, they would get a very narrow view of that culture. Even the food you got would not always be authentic. The book *Chop Suey Nation* (Hui, 2019) tells stories of many Asian families opening Chinese restaurants to make a living in small Canadian towns. They serve food they know that will be liked by White people, not necessarily food that is authentically Chinese. What if you befriended an Asian person, and you ate at each other's homes. What if you had frank conversations about the experiences they had. Perhaps by living in the neighborhood you would see first-hand what it was like for many of those families and communities. This is a way to be less of a tourist, and more of a participant in different communities. When people realize you are not just there for a visit and the photo opportunities, they will open up to you with their experiences and their world, because their world is now yours. The process now is more natural, organic, and egalitarian.

3.9   More Examples

In many cultural communities, there will be a token White friend who is there all of the time. A colleague who is a White woman had grown up and primarily been friends with South and East Asian people. She was dubbed the "Cauc to their Asian," and though she lived her life as a White woman, she had an intimate understanding of Asian cultural issues. A good friend of mine is a White Irish woman who converted to Islam. Though her perspective was initially very privileged, over time, and by spending time and making friends with people of color, she began to get the inside jokes she otherwise would have missed, meaning she had seen a side of the experience she missed initially when she was not a part of the community.

Cultural competence is not something that we obtain, and for which we are rewarded a diploma. It is about an ongoing process in a conversation, and there still may be differences and nuances that people do not get.

3.9.1   Comedians and Cultural Competence

Derald Wing Sue (2019) describes cross-cultural competence as engaging with, and advocating and negotiating for, people from different cultural perspectives than yourself. A critical example of this is the comedian Bill Burr, a White man. Through his comedy, he addresses topics that many White people are not always privy too. He has addressed the racism of White women, and Elvis Presley's cultural appropriation of the music of the Black community in the US; topics that demonstrate a nuanced understanding of issues that reflect the perspectives of and are typically spoken of more about in

Proximity to people and their experiences teaches us about different worldviews

communities of color. During his performances, he also talks about his wife, who is Black and from whom he learns. Burr, who is no stranger to controversial opinions, describes himself as stubborn. But being married to a Black woman, and having integrated her into not just his community but his family, his worldview has changed and his cultural competence improved. Through acceptance of his errors, his willingness to learn, and through embarrassing moments, he obtained a nuanced cultural experience of Black people, in particular Black women. This is a clear example showing that biases can be addressed, racism minimized, and cultural competence and trust achieved, regardless of perceived difference, the moment we recognize "the other" as a part of a larger human community.

Another comedian, Michelle Wolf, a White woman, also uses her proximity to people of color to address key issues of bias, racism, centering Whiteness, and what is colloquially known as "Karening" (a pejorative term used to describe a social phenomenon when White women unnecessarily and often violently express entitlement and privilege over people of color) in her comedic commentary. She openly describes her experiences of insight and awareness of her own privilege through the comparison of her partner who is a Black man, and uses that to encourage other White people to identify their privilege and engage in cultural humility.

The Canadian and American community tends to prefer Whiteness (although this preference is seen globally through manifestation of colorism and colonialism), and, according to research, to see White leaders more positively than leaders of color (Gundemir et al., 2014), but it is important to realize these perspectives are not static. As leaders of color remained longer in their roles, research found that perceptions of them shifted from negative to far more positive, equaling perceptions of White leaders. The same was also true about bias in children. Though White children who had no exposure to other people of color prior to school had a clear preference toward other White children, after 3 years of engagement with a more diverse student body, they began to relate to other students based on similar interests, not ethnicity (M. T. Williams et al., 2019). This demonstrates that exposure to, and engagement with, people we perceive as different, will allow us, over time, to establish increased relatability and compassion, because we see them as a part of our community. This, as noted many times before, must remain a very conscious process, otherwise the implicit nature of segregation and White supremacy remains consistently strong.

4

The Perspective of the Client

Now that we have discussed the perspective of the practitioner, we can turn our attention to understanding the perspective of the client. You will not understand your client's needs by addressing differences, but instead you should focus on the common challenges faced by clients of color from different cultural backgrounds.

Focusing on the perspective of the client as an outsider, or foreign to the practitioner, has typically been the hallmark of most cross-cultural models of practice (Hofstede, 2011; Meyer, 2016). However, taking this approach exotifies non-White cultures, and creates White culture as the standard with which to measure or compare those cultures. So that even if the views of people from different cultures are "respected," the approach still separates instead of unifying. The heart of any good relationship is the ability to relate, and find empathy. At best, taking this comparative exotic approach to cultures feels orientalist. It is, as Edward Said describes in *Orientalism* (Said, 2003), a situation in which Western cultures (and the people who make them up) are viewed as superior to Eastern cultures (and the people who make them up). Even though Eastern cultures (and any culture that is non-White) are romanticized, the measuring stick still remains, in a large part, White culture, which is privileged, as are people from that culture. Understandably, this process of getting to know others is not only racist, but promotes stereotypes, and leaves the practitioner of any cross-cultural practice unaware of their engagement in a working relationship, therapeutic or otherwise. This is why getting to know the client and their worldview occurs after the practitioner first identifies their worldview and perspective and their role in social constructs such as racism, orientalism, xenophobia, and colonialism. As Samuel Huntington points out in *The Clash of Civilizations* (Huntington, 1997), future wars will not be fought between countries, but rather between cultures. Taking a more egalitarian and empathy-based approach to cross-cultural relations is a more adept way of addressing the topic.

Given that people of color and those from nondominant cultures experience racism and discrimination so consistently, understanding the impact of these on worldviews is an essential first step to understanding the client, more than any tokenistic understanding of the window dressing of food and dress might be in traditional modes of cross-cultural competence.

If we recall how the tip for the practitioner was to reframe their perspective of who was in their community – people of color already do that and have done that for eons. They know more about the dominant cultural norms than those from dominant cultures know about theirs. In fact, they are also at risk for having internalized White values as their norm. As a result, they are more likely to empathize with you and understand your perspective, but you may not be able to understand theirs. This is a challenge they will experience, and you need to be aware of this in your understanding of their worldview. Not being aware puts the practitioner at risk of becoming the client, where the client is managing the needs of the practitioner.

In instances where the practitioner is White, clients often code switch to manage the fragility of the practitioner. When the practitioner is not White, there is often an assessment that occurs in which the client needs to determine what level of cultural and ethnic identity the practitioner has, to determine how honest they can be with them. In some cases, cultural congruence between the client and the practitioner is sought to minimize code switching and to increase trust. In other situations, there is a complete avoidance of cultural familiarity out of fear that the client's worldview clashes with their culture of origin.

Regardless of this, it is important to be aware that racism, orientalism, xenophobia, and colonialism lead clients to engage in one of the following:

1. Internalizing racism – acquiesce to a White-centered working relationship, diminishing their own cultural identity.
2. Placing barriers around issues essential to the working relationship, due to diminished trust and greater fear of judgment, reducing the effectiveness of the working relationship.

Cultural and ethnic identity development are important to consider in cross-cultural work

Depending on where someone is in the development of their cultural and ethnic identity, different problems can arise. Before proceeding further, it is important we consider the concept of ethnic and cultural identity development and how racism impacts that (Figure 1).

The model works on the premise that due to social problems such as racism, people of color or those from nondominant, non-White cultures are consistently in conflict, except for recent immigrants to Western countries. But the longer an immigrant of color stays in a country with a dominant White culture, or if they are born in that culture, then they are increasingly at odds with themselves. The more marginalized they are, the more they need to come to terms with ethnic and cultural identity, which is at odds with Whiteness as we know it today, or rather, White supremacy. The goal for a person of color or someone from a non-White, nondominant culture, is to move toward self-acceptance, without needing to change who they are, or without needing to adopt Whiteness into their identity to feel good about who they are. This, however, is a challenging and sometimes lofty goal, because marginalized people may often waffle back and forth, finding moments of resiliency, but often falling backward given the strength and prevalence of White supremacy.

This ethnic and cultural identity development, however, is often at odds with a Western cultural paradigm, or Whiteness. And at times, the greater the strength in cultural and ethnic identity, the greater the tension or White fragility, of people around that person of color or person from a nondominant culture. That tension can also occur in other people of color if they have strongly internalized Whiteness as the norm and expectation, or if they are working to remain safe from retaliation by remaining quiet about their

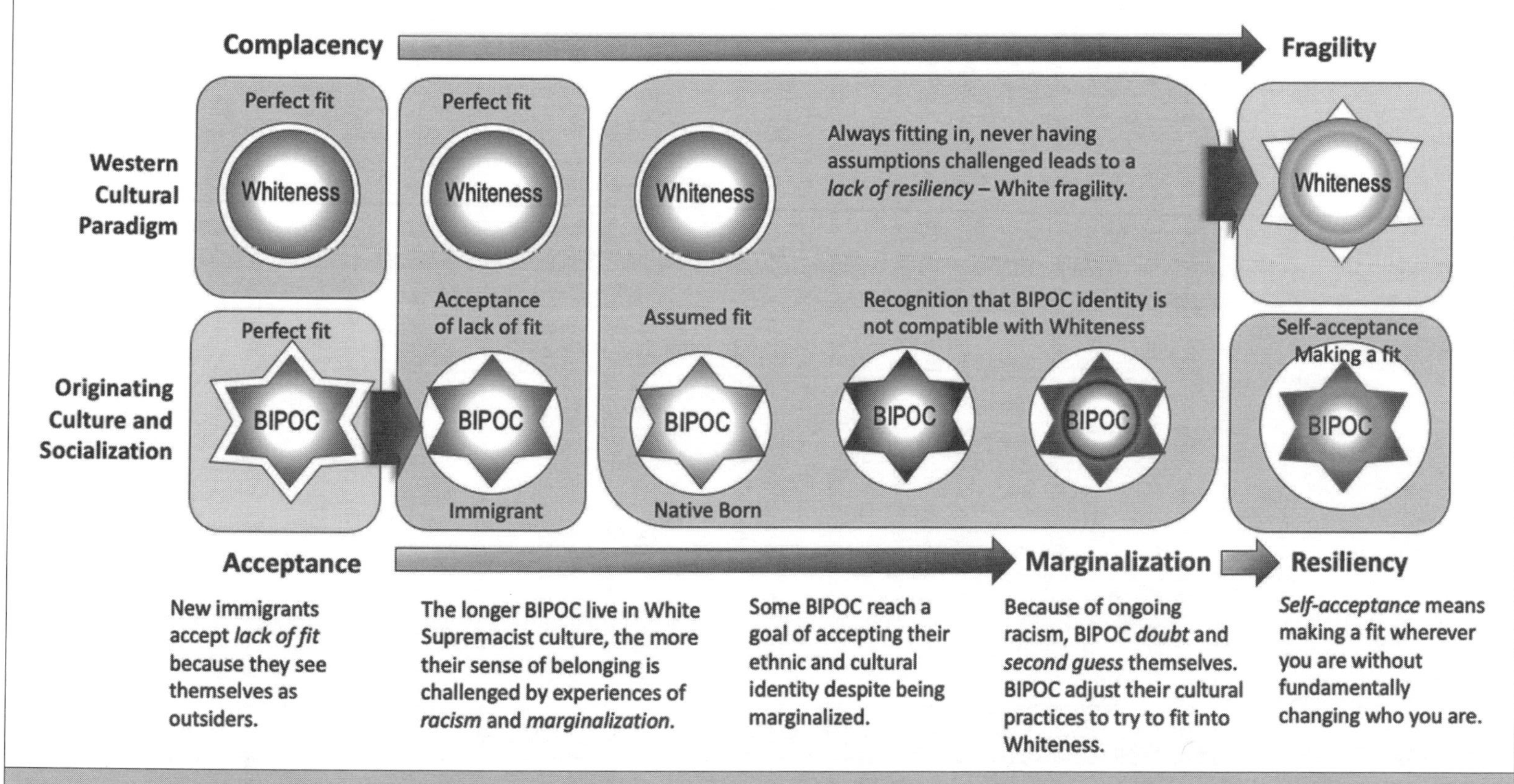

Figure 1. The impact of racism on social belonging and identity. BIPOC = Black, Indigenous, or people of color.

identity. It is important to understand that in a healthy cross-cultural working alliance, the stronger a non-White identity, the greater the likelihood old patterns of dominance may be threatened. The following issues are matters to consider when understanding the perspective of the client.

4.1   Assimilation and Cultural Identity

Assimilation should not be the goal for cross-cultural work

Being assimilated into a dominant culture does not result in psychologically healthy attitudes or a positive sense of self-worth. Yet this is a bias many will hold. There are two biases here when it comes to assimilation: (1) the bias of the therapist that a healthy individual is assimilated into the dominant culture; and (2) the bias of the client who believes that they will better by abandoning their culture and adopting a White culture, the dominant culture. Both work from the frame of reference that centers Whiteness and White culture as dominant.

A healthy identity is one that is self-determined. Though many therapists might agree with this, it is not always as easily experienced or understood when it comes to cultural self-acceptance, but is instead usually applied to individuals who chose to let go of their cultures.

Though many may assume cultural ideals from the culture or family of origin are archaic or not in alignment with "modern values," this belief is based on misinformation and upholds elements of orientalism and racism (Said, 2003). We often believe that self-determined choices to let go of culture are truly self-determined, but the choice to sustain a cultural belief or practice is due to pressure from family and community and a sign of oppression. What is ignored, however, are the racist and xenophobic cultures of White supremacy that influence the choices people make, and falsely assume to be their own. When White supremacy is so strong and so profound in our culture, and so heavily rewarded (by acceptance and social praise), it pushes or forces people of color and those from nondominant cultures to abandon or modify cultural practice and beliefs to fit or clash less with Whiteness. When there is constant punishment (e.g., microaggressions, systemic racism preventing cultural practice, etc.) of individuals who sustain their cultural, religious, ethnic self, of course, that will influence "choice." But in this situation then, the word "choice" or self-determination, must be used loosely, and understood to be influenced by systems of oppression, where the choice to adopt a dominant culture is, at best, a means of self-preservation.

When cultural and ethnic identity is compromised because of social pressure (keeping in mind that the client may not always be aware of this compromised identity), it is important practitioners have a better understanding of the reasons for those "choices" are made. Sometimes it is not about oppression, and sometimes it is, but in order to be able to differentiate between the two, you need to identify your own bias and help the client identify theirs. If you assume that somebody is automatically healthy because they have detached themselves from a family or culture, when a cultural standard the practitioner belongs to is not a system that is family oriented, then that is not the healthiest thing. It also then forces and colonializes the choices of the practitioner onto the client.

4.2 Internalized Racism and Blaming Themselves or Their Own Cultures

It is not uncommon for people from smaller cultural communities to experience frustration with some aspects of their community. These kinds of challenges are common in rural White communities in Canada and the US. But consider the example of a woman who is very angry at people in her ethnic community and has made some assumptions about that community. It would be the job of the therapist to not automatically rush in to support her criticism of her community. Although we want to hear and acknowledge the client, we also want to be able to challenge her. Even in examples where frustrations are far more serious, as in the example below, blaming an entire group of people due to the misbehavior of one needs to be challenged.

4.2.1 Example

Practitioner: *Tell me why you feel that way about your community?*
Client: *Well, I had this experience where I was abused by a man from my community. And this was someone who was a leader in the community that I was raised in.*
Practitioner: [After validating the experiences and emotions tied to the abuse, realizes it would be helpful to determine if the abuse occurred due to culture, or was simply an abuse of power, which could and does occur in all communities] *Do you have other experiences with people from your community? What could the abuse be tied to? Is that one person the entire community, are there people that might challenge that view? Do you know if abuse like this occurs in other communities? Are there people in your community you trust who you could involve to support you?*

I have seen numerous clients who hold very negative views about their ethnic and cultural communities. Because the problem they experienced occurred in their community, and because of White supremacist views that White culture does not have these problems, the individual will often attribute the problem to the culture. What they do not recognize is that some of the challenges in their community exist across different cultures. This is an issue of humanity, not culture.

My parents own a Middle Eastern food shop, and I grew up working there. People from our community would frequently come in, challenge the prices and try to bargain. The haggling became very frustrating for my parents. The perspective I developed as a child was that our community was cheap and insensitive to the work that went into running a business. What I realized over time is that his haggling occurs in many communities, including many White cultural communities as well.

As I grew up, I recognized that I heard people from other communities say similar things about their community, and I recognized it was not a pattern that was exclusive to me or my culture. My community had patterns and problems tied to it that were common in many smaller communities, including many Eastern cultures, and sometimes rural Canadian and American culture.

4.2.2   Example

I recall a very public critic of Islam, who came from the Muslim community, who in one interview described a very traumatic experience in which her father (who claimed to be religious) was very emotionally and verbally abusive toward her and her mother. At the same time, she also recalled experiencing significant racism when her mother made a well-known North American favorite, Rice Krispie squares, and was criticized by those in the White school and student community around her for not making them properly. Though I am not sure she recognized it at the time, she conflated an abuser with a culture or system of beliefs. It is common for abusers to use systems of beliefs (Eastern or Western) to control their victims. But this public figure also did not identify the impact of racism in that interview. Now because she was criticizing Islam, and was a Muslim herself, many Islamophobes cherished and promoted her talks, using the impact of abuse on numerous fronts to promote White supremacist and Islamophobic discourse. I wonder where this prominent speaker was in her ethnic and cultural identity development. Though her criticism of her abusive father was very much valid, was her assumption that all of Islam had misogynistic views of women, deeming them worthy of abuse? If you believe this, I encourage you to review your biases about Muslims and Islam and ensure your awareness of women's rights violations in specific communities are not conflated with the values of an entire group, and would ask you to also look at and examine the flagrant violations of women's rights around the world, including in North America. The one-sided approach does often speak to bias, internalized racism, but also the delicate and important issue of how that client might see themselves in relation to their cultural and ethnic identity and community.

4.3   Self-Critical Beliefs

One of the critical components of cross-cultural therapy and removing microaggressions is making sure that your clients are not microaggressing against themselves.

In our community, there was a young girl who had arrived as a refugee with her family. Their culture and ethnicity are unimportant, as this could have been any person or family from any community of color or from any non-dominant culture. Due to some challenges she was having, the family sought out therapeutic support for her, from a White therapist. The client, a teenage girl, complained about her family, which is actually not an uncommon teenage issue. The assumption made by the therapist was that the restrictions were due to the culture and religion of the community this girl belonged to, and that her cultural community that she came from was dominant and controlling (a stereotype often applied to that community). Deciding to play the role of a White savior, the therapist, in an extreme move, took the child into their own home and refused to let the family have access to her.

The family, recent refugees, did not know what to do, and approached many people within the community to assist but were leery about approaching professionals outside of the community after this experience. They also were fearful about approaching government agencies or child protection services because they were afraid that the government agency would support and validate the White professionals and there was a fear that their daughter would be taken away permanently. As time progressed, the teenager actually had a psychotic break and some of her difficulties were eventually attributed to early psychosis. In this case, the bias, and I would say macro aggression was so powerful, that it prevented a very well qualified professional from actually looking for the symptoms of a psychiatric illness. Instead, the therapist blamed the child's culture, when a more reasonable and medically supported diagnosis was available. Furthermore, the bias engaged in an alienation of the child from the family, removing long-standing social support from the child.

Fears such as these from marginalized communities often prevent them from seeking care or services from professionals who are not culturally congruent (Babu, 2017). And based on numerous experiences like the one described above, these individuals are justified in their suspicion and distrust of authority figures.

4.4 Internalized Racism, Identity Hiding, and Code Switching

For many, the problem is not about avoiding cross-cultural engagement, but rather hiding elements of who they are. Code switching becomes the method by which some people of color and those from nondominant cultures survive because of the threat posed by being authentic.

Understand code switching as a cultural coping or survival mechanism

Many people talk about code switching. It results when people from a minority culture, or people from a less dominant culture or people of color around a dominant culture, switch their cultural identity to appease the dominant culture. This influences how they talk, what they choose to eat, how they present themselves, what clothing they choose to wear, and how they choose to wear their hair.

People of color and people from nondominant cultural communities talk about code switching on a regular basis. It results from internalized racism that centers Whiteness and White culture. When people of color encounter a helping professional, there is a strong likelihood that they are code switching. If you are a professional who is White or from a dominant culture, and you are centering everything around your assumptions, you are perpetuating a need for people of color and those from nondominant cultures to code switch, because you are not really allowing that person to be truly who they are. If a person is not aware or lacks insight into their own code switching, and if they have normalized a White supremacist point of view, they will go along with you, furthering a devaluation of who they are and of what their cultural and ethnic identity is, and you are not helping with their mental health or anything for that matter if you do not address this issue.

One of the greatest barriers I would say exists to cross-cultural competence is the failure to center the client. This is why, in some cases, people who are from nondominant cultural communities, prefer professionals who are culturally congruent. They look for people who have had similar experiences, because they "get it," and understand the nuances of a cultural perspective, including being marginalized, without the need to explain that experience, or the fear that a misunderstanding of that cultural norm would lead to alienation or in some cases, active harm to the client.

The opposite can also indicate a problem. If a client says they prefer to avoid seeing someone who is culturally congruent, that may suggest to you that there is an issue they may have with their own cultural community. And in many cases, they have already moved away from their cultural community and do not want to be judged for doing so. For many White practitioners, or those from a dominant White culture, this would not be an issue, and may in fact, be rewarded as an individual "progressing" and making self-determined choices. What is missed, however, is the critical component of internalized racism, along with awareness of the diversity of experiences that can be had by people in a community.

A very clear preference for a practitioner from the same cultural background, or a practitioner from a different cultural community, should be diagnostic in giving you an impression of approximately where an individual of color may be in their own cultural and ethnic identity development.

4.5   The Elephant in the Room

Be prepared to have complex and difficult discussions about ethnic and cultural identity development

A discussion about where someone is in their ethnic and cultural identity development can be difficult. This is difficult enough when practitioner and client are both people of color or from nondominant cultures; it becomes even more complex when the practitioner is White and the client is not. Furthermore, when ethnic and cultural identity development are a non-issue for a White practitioner (due to White privilege), how then can therapists address or assess this issue with clients who do not have that same privilege.

The answer is not that one needs to assess or diagnose the issue, but rather to raise the issue, identify any privilege they have about not needing to address this for themselves, and recognize that a history of White supremacy tends to cause these issues for many people of color. The response may be defensive, but without raising the issue, it is ignored completely. And ignoring the issue leads to complacency in racism and not acknowledging ethnic and cultural identity development.

Illustration 4.

Due to the anxiety tied to issues of racism and cross-cultural competence, examples discussed so far may be difficult to digest. But if we consider related issues within a White population, the issues become clearer. Let's take the example of a straight White male therapist working with another White man who happens to be gay and in a gay relationship. If the straight man avoids discussing nuances of being gay, including gay sex, gay romance, and issues of coming out or not, because they are afraid of misunderstanding them, making errors, or even due to their own discomfort and homophobia, how can the issues the client is facing be addressed? Furthermore, we live in a world that is generally heteronormative, and it produces much internalized homophobia in many people who are gay, bi, or queer. Ignoring the impact of homophobia and internalized homophobia with a queer client would in essence be supporting homophobia by avoidance of the necessary issues. In this case, the practitioner's own perspective needs to be addressed, their own challenges brought up, and their willingness to learn also noted, in order for the necessary issues to be properly assessed and addressed.

In the same way, one may not need to be from the same cultural or ethnic background as a client, in order to identify their own worldviews, deficits in knowledge, and willingness to learn, so as to then address similar issues with the client. Ignoring the elephant in the room only forces it to get bigger when it comes to ethnic and cultural identity development.

In some cases, our biases are contradictory. For example, what we feel uncomfortable talking about with one person (e.g., sexual fetishization with a gay man of color), we not only feel comfortable talking about, but also projecting our value system on others (e.g., suggesting a Muslim woman who may practice premarital abstinence from sex, date more). In both cases, the cultural supremacy of White heteronormative culture are centered (Illustration 4).

4.6   Supporting Human Rights While Remaining Anti-Racist

It is sometimes difficult to support an individual and their rights, while remaining anti-racist and being aware of the internalized racism your client experiences (as well as the White supremacist views you may hold as a practitioner). For example, this is often the case when working with issues tied to women's rights. It is not uncommon for practitioners to equate women's rights with the emancipation of women from cultural norms. On the one hand, as helping professionals, we need to be able to support and defend human rights, which include women's rights in all cultures. On the other hand, we need to be mindful that we are not hiding behind that defense to bash another culture or promote a stereotypical view of a particular group of people, and the false ideology that as a Western society, we are better at maintaining women's rights (Nelson, 2021). Furthermore, it is essential that we do not help clients internalize racism and xenophobia about their own cultural and ethnic identity as the means by which we help them "escape" their culture and ethnic identity. This is especially common when working with Muslim women; stereotypes about them being victims can negatively impact their cultural and ethnic identity. In situations where there are clear human rights violations, a practitioner can be helpful without blaming or bashing an entire culture. The practitioner must look for examples of human rights supporters from within the culture, and also point out human rights violations in the dominant culture. Take for example the violation of Indigenous women's rights in Canada, by White men, where the issue of missing and murdered Indigenous women is an epidemic concern (Nelson, 2021), and yet it is broadly ignored by the dominant society (Hayes, 2023).

Many clients are vulnerable and question elements of their identity; this is especially likely if their cultural identity is directly or indirectly referred to as backward or barbaric (Barber, 2015). Casting aside one's cultural identity is more likely – and the impact of racism more impactful – on these vulnerable populations. In cases like these, helping professionals are in fact harmful, and building infrastructure for a fragile identity based on the supremacy of someone the client is not. Being anti-racist, culturally sensitive, and promoting human rights can occur simultaneously, and it is important that all of those issues are addressed by any practitioner aiming for cross-cultural competence. Ignoring cultural relevance and value of any group, while trying to save someone from their identity and values, promotes White saviorism, which will be explored in the next chapters (Sections 6.4 and 7.4) in the context of Gender and Female Empowerment) where it can commonly occur, and as noted in examples earlier in this book (see Illustration 4).

4.7 Multiple Contributors to Cultural Identity

One way in which identity can be explored is through the multiple factors that contribute to it. For some people, there are clear lines separating culture, religion, and ethnicity. There are also numerous other factors including immigration, migration trauma, and even political history. All of these and more may contribute to a worldview that together can create endless permutations and combinations. For other clients, these elements are all fused together. The less informed they are about their identity, the more fused these three elements become. Addressing issues in one area automatically impacts the others. The more informed a client is of their identity, the greater clarity they have in identifying which belief and worldview came from which area. This creates some fluidity in identity and can allow clients to develop their own self-determined identity without needing to resort to White supremacy or abandoning their cultural identity fully (Illustration 5).

Cultural identity is nuanced and multifactorial

Illustration 5.

One of the ways in which I encourage clients to better accept their identity is to look for perspectives and solutions to some of their dilemmas (tied to internalized racism and what might appear to be a cultural conflict) within their own cultural perspective. So, for example, a client of mine was so put off by their cultural community, seeing them as "backward gossip mongers" that they decided instead to adopt the "Western" value of "minding your own business." What occurred here was a transition from a more collective group mentality to resolving problems in their community, to her belief that

"White people" were more successful because they were more individualistic. White supremacy and internalized racism caused this client to want to dispense with her cultural identity, presuming it to be problematic. When I asked if those people she presumed to be gossip mongers were helpful to her in her life, she was able to agree they were, and she was able to find value in her community. When I pointed out situations in which she felt abandoned by White colleagues not wanting to get involved in an issue, she realized that individualistic perspectives also did not always work for her. This allowed her to see that the labels of individualistic and community-based values were not always stereotypical, and it allowed her to be less critical of her own community and thus herself. Problems became just problems, rather than character flaws of an entire group of people. It is also important to realize that cultural and ethnic community carries with it its own accumulated wisdom and learning. Culturally sensitive practitioners will need to look into these sources for solutions that account for and incorporate a culturally sensitive resolution.

A practitioner cannot always assume that a value-based judgment a person of color makes about their community is accurate, or based on a perspective not influenced by prejudice. Questioning, asking, and learning are essential on an ongoing basis to understand, but also to encourage, clients to review their own internalized racism. The development of cultural and ethnic identity takes time, effort, and strife. Not mentioning where someone is in their cultural and ethnic identity development limits any possibility for discussing how racism has impacted their ability to accept who they are culturally and ethnically.

Sometimes when somebody is not comfortable with their ethnic and cultural identity, it is a service to them to help identify the automatic triggers that result from a lack of comfort in their own cultural and ethnic identity. A need to be White that is recognized by a person of color can result in defensiveness. Sometimes this tension can be increased if the person pointing this out is White; at other times, it can be increased if it is a person of color. Having a person who has not experienced marginalization point out a process they have the privilege of not needing to go through can be frustrating. In contrast, being evaluated by a practitioner of color on where they are in their ethnic and cultural identity can feel judgmental. These discussions need to happen slowly and cautiously, and they should occur once rapport is developed. People who are comfortable with their ethnic and cultural identity development are not going to have an issue being identified as having a different experience (in contrast to the assumption or any statement suggesting they are foreign, which is a microaggression), because they already know that their experience is different.

4.8   The Challenge

The challenge is double edged: Practitioners are aiming to improve their cross-cultural skills while being mindful of their own bias, but also while recognizing that one needs to help identify the bias and or internalized racism or internalized discrimination that clients from cultural communities express or feel.

At times, the Western way is not the best way. What we often believe to be professional, or evidence-based, sometimes reflects a bias toward the perspective of a culturally dominant community. Take for example the concept of individualism versus collectivism. It is not uncommon for many therapists to advocate individualism for a client whose cultural perspective is collectivist. Forcing an individualistic approach on a person whose social support system thrives on collectivist values undermines the system that they grew up in and removes their social support system.

Practitioners need to weigh the pros and cons in those circumstances, respecting their client's cultural and ethnic identity development and discussing how to achieve a balanced approach that works well for that individual without the automatic assumption that the practitioner's cultural perspective (the White measuring stick) is automatically best.

People of color or those from nondominant cultures sometimes let go of certain elements of themselves because it is easy (and the truth is acting White and assuming the norms of the dominant culture are easier than sustaining a cultural identity). Therapists can support the rejection of the White perspective, helping provide the cognitive and emotional infrastructure needed for healthy and functional identity development, self-esteem, and security.

Because it is easy, many people will code switch or completely remove any element of cultural identity from themselves. Yet, interestingly, doing so does not remove experiences of racism and marginalization. A culturally competent therapist will, over time, begin to recognize the things many people of color and those from nondominant cultures attempt to minimize the experience of racism and feel more accepted (Casimir, 2020; Dickens, 2019; Hall & Nilep, 2015). Often these attempts to fit into the dominant culture come at great cost. Examples include Whitening or anglicizing of names, the celebration of White holidays and the minimizing of the holidays of the nondominant culture, the bleaching of skin and straightening of hair, the vilification of fellow community members of color, the simplification of food choices, choosing not to disclose living in a multigenerational household, hiding religious practices, adjusting clothing preferences, presenting fake histories in romantic relationships or even creating false narratives about relationships entirely, and the adoption of beauty standards associated with White people.

Though this is not an exhaustive list of things people to do code switch, or "acculturate" into White culture just to attempt to reduce discrimination, it is easy to imagine how responding to all these elements of our identity can be exhausting. If your response to these issues is silence or a lack of acknowledgement as a practitioner, you do your clients a tremendous disservice. The challenge for White practitioners is to address these issues without flaunting their privilege or trying to reshape the identity of their clients who are people of color.

4.9   Cultural Safety

Many clients will avoid practitioners who are not culturally congruent, to avoid being marginalized by them. The need for cultural safety and the lack of it in many professions is keenly noticed by people of color and those from nondominant cultures (Curtis et al., 2019). In some situations, even diagnoses are wrongly applied due to negative or false perceptions of certain cultural issues. I recall a colleague who once shared that their family members were informally diagnosed by another White colleague as likely having personality disorders. But this colleague of color reminded the White colleague, they were not personality disordered, it was just that boundaries varied culturally, as did styles of expression. But for some time after, my colleague found herself questioning if her family members had personality disorders, even though there was almost no conflict in their family, and no evidence of illness.

Cultural safety isn't always identified, but it is an important contributor to a safe working relationships. Imagine avoiding psychological care, fearful of your culture being misinterpreted, or even the fear that you may be separated from family. It is for this reason many people seek out cultural congruence. If they do see someone who is not culturally congruent, but who is a person of color, they may feel some form of congruence. In other situations where people of color who are seeking cultural safety but cannot find a culturally congruent practitioner, they may go to that practitioner anyway simply because no one else is available. In this case, being aware of that need and addressing it up front is essential in developing trust.

4.10   Cultural Congruence

I would like to revisit the example of the Filipino adolescent referred by my White mentor. Remember that my colleague was one of the most pleasant and kind people you would meet, and that many, including myself, would refer to him as a saint. Though issues of internalized racism mingled with social anxiety for this client, it was an interaction with her father that clued me into the issue of cultural congruence for the trust needed in this client. The father stopped me 1 day after our session to say he was happy that I was seeing his daughter instead of my colleague, "the White guy," because he felt that I would understand the issues and the family more than my colleague would. Put simply, he liked me "because you are like us."

I am not Filipino or Catholic, but seeing a person of color was important for this father and his family. The fear of being misunderstood, the fear of judgment, and in some cases, very real concern about social repercussions (Cénat et al., 2021) reduce trust for many people of color in White professionals. In my practice, it is not uncommon that I get requests from people from my cultural and religious community across the country to see them or family members virtually, as they state, clearly, they "cannot trust White" professionals with the vulnerable issues of mental health.

In some cases, I've seen a fair number of "White" clients, who are from Eastern and Southern European cultures who, although White, do not see themselves culturally as White. Like the Filipino father above, they have often said to me, "Your culture is like ours and you understand us and our ways. So, we would like to see you."

The sentiment of wanting someone from the same or similar culture, or someone with *cultural congruency*, is a phenomenon well documented in research (Ertl et al.,2019; Huey et al., 2014; Ilagan & Heatherington, 2022; Kim, 2018; Owen, 2011), and it is the common experience of many people of color. This does not mean they will not see professionals who are White, but their trust is low, and people of color and people from different cultural communities remain guarded in therapy and other working relationships.

Cultural congruence doesn't mean a 100% overlap in identities, but rather greater similarity and thus comfort

4.11 Vulnerability

Remember that not everyone has the privilege to be vulnerable

The concept of vulnerability is lauded as a key to personal growth by figures as well known as Brene Brown (2011) to large therapeutic professional groups such as Functional Analytic Psychotherapy (Holman et al., 2017). Figures such as Brene Brown have built entire professional empires on this concept. In fact, experts focusing on the "simplicity" of therapeutic relationships rely heavily on the concept of vulnerability. Yet, it is clear the concept of vulnerability as a key to success is clearly tied to White privilege. Carey Yazeed (2021a) minces no words when she talks about how Brown's discussion of vulnerability does not reflect Yazeed's experience as a Black woman. In Yazeed's article, her book, and in a recent podcast with myself (Abdulrehman, 2022), she discusses how vulnerability was not only something she did not have the privilege to engage in when in professional relationships; furthermore, when she attempted to do so, she was attacked for it. Many people of color and people from nondominant cultures have a very difficult time shaking stereotypes they are shackled with.

Derald Sue (2010) reports that stereotypical themes or biases still exist about certain groups of people, including the association of criminality with Black people, and sinfulness with gay people. I find similar results in my own BOB data (Abdulrehman & Clara, 2023). National polls of Canadians have documented the widespread belief that Indigenous people were obstacles to social and economic growth (Aboriginal Peoples Television Network Poll [APTN], 2016). It makes sense then that we believe what is commonly stated by people from marginalized cultures and people of color, who feel gaslit when they seek out vulnerability and are instead shackled with harm and trauma. Experiences such as these occur on a regular basis for many people of color and those of nondominant cultures, and it is essential that any practitioner working with such clients is aware of those experiences and the impact and ability to be honest, and vulnerable, with those with whom they do not have cultural and ethnic congruence.

In some cases, when people of color hold biases and police others from their own communities, challenges have occurred even when cultural congruence has existed, making trust and full disclosure even harder. Many of the examples already given occurred when racism was actually perpetrated by other people of color. This suggests that regardless of the ethnicity and culture of the practitioner, clients who are from these populations may still need time and the development of trust and the understanding that they will not be harmed by you, in order for the work to truly begin.

4.12 Politicized Identities and Psychological Checkpoints

The themes of bias and stereotypes tied to certain groups of people, as noted above, can often be linked with *politicized identities*. Because much of the work world feels uncomfortable addressing "political issues," substantive political issues are often ignored. That means working relationships in therapy, health, finance, etc., all require the ability to be aware of how culture, ethnicity, and even religion become political. This makes actual people political hot buttons and triggers. When working with people of color and those from nondominant, and even colonized cultures, the ability to address this and be aware of the nuances of how identity is politicized are critically important. This includes how the identity of the practitioner can serve as a trigger for stress, and reluctance to be honest or vulnerable. It also explains why clients may code switch and hide elements of their identity and viewpoints, because of the fear of being labeled as political if they actually bring up issues of life that have been of central importance to them.

For example, when people of color typically politicized and stereotyped as violent and barbaric (e.g., Muslims, Arabs, Palestinians) raise issue of injustice against their own people (e.g., opposing occupation and human rights violations of Palestinians), they are further stereotyped and seen as sympathetic to terrorism and face consequences, even in academic settings (Macintosh, 2023). The consequences of speaking out against racism and injustice toward politicized people of color also extends to White allies in the professional world, such as with the well-known academic Norman Finkelstein (Abraham, 2011), clarifying that concepts of free speech and academic freedoms do not keep people safe from racism. This trap of racism leaves people of color (and their allies) to either accept marginalization and inequity or face consequences of political identities and stereotypes; both producing actual risk to quality of life and safety. Activists such as Nelson Mandela and Angela Davis are important historic examples as both were labeled terrorists and imprisoned for seeking social justice, but we know this problem still occurs today. You must ensure you are not trapping people of color due to your own biases and beliefs that sustain your power and dominance over them.

> **We often can't avoid our identities being politicized**

The threat of politicized identities in people of color produces a unique challenge for clients of color similar to code switching. With code switching, people of color need to adjust their behavior to appear or pass as culturally White (assimilated into Western culture); in contrast, pressuring from a practitioner to have a client disavow their advocacy for human rights of people of color is what I call a "psychological checkpoint." More specifically, to be allowed access to a service, to professional trust, and to basic human rights, people of color are first required to disavow the rights of their own people (or risk being called a terrorist or terrorist sympathizer) and prioritize the rights and freedoms of White people over their own in order to be offered service, safety, or even simple credibility. This ironically diffuses the point of advocating for one's own community and safety, and re-establishes power for those with White privilege. These checkpoints, physical infrastructures that prevent oppressed people in Apartheid states from moving freely and without bother through their own communities, also continue to be reflected in psychological or cognitive infrastructures of people and thus cultures or societies that claim to not be racist (e.g., Canada, the US, and other Western countries). Like the unnecessary physical checkpoints in Apartheid states, psychological checkpoints create a false sense of fragility/victimhood in the person administering the checkpoint, are meant to demean, create barriers to everyday necessary tasks, humiliate an oppressed population, and sustain a dominance and power of White people over people of color (all under the guise of security, suggesting oppressed people of color are violent and unsafe by nature); but do so behaviorally. They also deflect from the point of advocacy being made by the oppressed person of color, and redirect attention and victimhood to the oppressor and/or the person with greater privilege and power based on ethnicity and dominant cultural status (e.g., Whiteness). They occur not only between practitioner and client, but also in what appear to be egalitarian relationships, including between colleagues (where power disparities exist based on racism), and even in the media as a style of discourse when interviewing people of color. When considering racism, we must always be thoughtful of how physical infrastructures of racism in the past, remain alive and well in psychological infrastructures we internalize today, conscious or not. We must ensure we do not gatekeep our services only to people who align with White supremacy, or even simply for the purpose of sustaining a power dynamic for a sense of security based on White fragility. Whereas it is not uncommon that professionals of color provide service to people who are racist (at their own psychological cost for the sake of professional and humanitarian obligation), all practitioners must not gatekeep service or reduce quality of service to clients who do not hold prioritizing White lives and safety over the safety and lives of people of color. It is lastly important to realize that psychological checkpoints play an important role in gaslighting people of color, which can be a significant contributing factor to internalized racism and consequential behaviors such as code switching.

5

A Culturally Sensitive Working Relationship and Social Justice

Once we are able to address the biases of the practitioner, and the biases and worldview of the client, we can focus on the combination of those two in a culturally sensitive working alliance, while being mindful of the importance of social justice.

It is difficult to consider a culturally sensitive working relationship while ignoring the importance of social justice. The heart of cultural sensitivity is to ensure there is justice – or at least an understanding of how a lack of social justice could influence someone's life. This is the quintessential component to trust across the lines of ethnic and cultural disparities that exist in a White supremacist world.

If we consider that White supremacy is the centering of White culture, White people, and White perspectives in all elements of life in many parts of the Western world, we realize this ultimately creates a power dynamic that elevates White people above all others. The elevation creates a preference for, and gives benefits to, White people more than people of color and those from nondominant cultures. It also creates a stratification providing more power and dominance for White people. Even when White people advocate for equal rights of people of color, they are more likely to be successful than people of color themselves, due to White privilege (Collins, 2017).

This power dynamic is an undercurrent in many or most cross-cultural relationships, including in working relationships. This is a challenging concept to come to terms with, because we often prefer to believe we have come further as a society and individually when it comes to abolishing the stratification of people and the related power dynamics that come with racism, but sadly that is not the case. As mentioned earlier, without an active mindfulness and vigilant response to decenter Whiteness in our day-to-day lives, the perspectives of people of color and those from nondominant cultures remains secondary. Ignoring this fact in any helping relationship, creates a complacency and sustains the status quo of this power dynamic between White people and people of color. The following sections cover how that occurs and how it can be reduced.

5.1   Transference and Countertransference

Psychotherapists are taught to be mindful of how clients may transfer emotions about other people and situations onto them. We also learn how we as therapists may get caught up in a relationship and counter transfer feelings about other circumstances back toward the client. In situations in which we work with victims of sexual abuse, it is commonplace for us to consider the impact of the gender of the perpetrator on the therapeutic relationship and how the impact of the gender of the therapist might influence therapeutic processes and outcomes. Outside of the world of racism, it becomes easy for many to understand how life experiences and the relationships our clients have outside the therapy room affect the relationship between a therapist and a client. Being thoughtful about how racism impacts our clients, and how it interacts with the ethnicity, culture, and perceived power of the therapist, is no different. It should be considered in exactly the same way and be dealt with as any trauma would be.

Racism and bias can impact transference and countertransference

There is considerable research confirming that racism (systemic or otherwise) creates trauma in people of color (M. T. Williams et al., in press). Reviewing Chapter 4 alone makes it clear that the impact of racism is profound. In the same way we are thoughtful and considerate to issues related to the trauma (realized or not by the client) while not patronizing the client, so is it necessary for a culturally sensitive working alliance.

5.2   The Good Immigrant

There is safety and value in people of color not bringing up concerns – You do not want to reinforce this

One of the key ways in which immigrants, people of color, and those from nondominant cultures gain privilege, which means economic and social growth, is by "playing nice." The "good immigrant" myth applies not only to immigrants, but people of color in general, in that they are seen as less desirable unless they work hard, integrate into a dominant culture, and behave themselves according to the rules set and managed by the White world (Shukla et al., 2020). However, the ability to be a "good immigrant" is tied to the difficult and simultaneous ability to remain silent, prospering with the few scraps given to people of color, accepting the idea that the Western world (America, Canada, the UK, and Australia) has been good to them, and publicly acknowledging that they have been able to achieve, with the permission of White people, what they could not get "back home." Any voicing of dissent to the challenge of racism, or the commonly held belief and experiences in any community of color that they needed to work infinitely harder than White people to achieve a fraction of their success, is met with platitudes and accusations of being ungrateful, and even unpatriotic. A fellow senior colleague, who is Black, once quipped at a conference that the only reason they were afforded space at some tables was because they were perceived to be a "Good N-word." They were perceived to be agreeable, and not someone who would challenge the status quo set by White leaders. When people of color who push back against these rules are seen as more difficult, then the doors to privilege begin to close. As an example, Indigenous people often do not obtain the same privileges because they do not play by the rules set by White colonialism and as such are deemed challenging and barriers to social progress (APTN, 2016).

In any professional working relationship, including therapy, there is pressure to be "good immigrants" or "good N-words." In the Black American community, the offensive term "Uncle Tom" refers to any person of color who betrays their cultural and ethnic allegiance to be more servile to White people. The existence of the term, regardless of how offensive it is, speaks to the sense of betrayal that communities of color feel when people give up or "sell out" their identity and culture to maintain the comfort of a White majority. And yet, it is clear not doing so comes at great risk, and so people of color are placed in a double bind: submit to maintaining White comfort at the expense of your own psychological well-being and be ostracized by your community, or disrupt White supremacy, colonialism, orientalism, and any other system that maintains disparity and be heavily punished for it. The risk of otherwise being direct about the challenges faced in life experience can often result in the punishment. Kenneth Roth, a White Jewish man, and one of America's top attorneys, speaking out on human rights and being anti-Apartheid for Palestinians, was denied a fellowship at Harvard (Aljazeera, 2023). Despite carrying the privilege of being White, highly educated, and a globally known advocate for human rights, being Jewish (from a nondominant culture) and advocating for people of color, led to the loss of his privileges. Roth is but one of countless examples of such punishments, and one can only imagine what would have occurred if he had not been White.

In a working culturally sensitive relationship, a practitioner must remember that they may not be getting the full truth of the client's perspective, due to fear of reprisal. It is only when trust is established and the client fully feels they will not be punished for stepping outside the role of a good person of color that they will disclose the full extent of their perspectives and needs, and their view of the quality of relationship with the practitioner. It is not an uncommon experience that people of color and those from nondominant cultures shield or keep from their White friends and colleagues the actual experiences they have with racism and marginalization for fear that they would not be understood or concern they may be accused of playing the race card, only because their White friends and colleagues do not see racism because they are blinded by their own White privilege. Despite racism and discrimination being openly talked about in today's society, I still maintain that due to the punishment associated with talking about those experiences, the extent of the presence of racism is still a well-kept secret in the Western world.

Despite efforts made by a White practitioner, unless their reputation for being an anti-racist advocate precedes them, developing a culturally sensitive working alliance will take some time. If the practitioner is a person of color, or from a nondominant culture, they must consider issues tied to the perceived privileges they carry, especially if they pass as White, or if they appear to be centering Whiteness, or if they are perceived by the client to be a "coconut." When being treated by or working with a coconut, the client will not see the practitioner as an ally or a relatable person, but instead a potential spy or police officer who enforces Whiteness among other people of color.

Consider the Tuskegee Syphilis Study authorized by the US Public Health Service, which is often implicated as a cause of medical mistrust among African Americans. The extensive decades-long deception of Black participants by White researchers would not have been possible without the key role of Black nurse Eunice Rivers Laurie, who created a bridge of trust between the research subjects and the medical staff (Hermann, 2000). As such, clients of color may be concerned that clinicians of color are simply tools of the establishment.

Practitioners who are people of color or from nondominant communities need also to identify this power differential and ensure that any inherent internalized version does not influence or alter their professional opinion or responsibility. An example of this, often seen in my own practice, occurs when I have made suggestions for reduced alcohol consumption due to mental health vulnerabilities. I have had clients push back, believing I was promoting a Muslim agenda. In other cases where I have worked with White veterans who worked in the Middle East, trust was often hard to come by, as they often initially perceived me as the "enemy." But even more simply, in everyday society, White people have more power, and it is not uncommon for people of color to have had less exposure to those social circles, as many White people tend to socialize with other White people (Cox et al., 2016). The intimacy that comes with a helping relationship can be a unique and disarming experience where they are challenged or even when advice is accepted.

5.3   Intercultural–Intracultural Conflict and Power Imbalances

What the description in the previous section suggests is that issues of hierarchy, power, and even colorism and intercultural conflict can occur within any working or helping professional relationship, just as they do in the everyday world. Consider the internal cultural conflict of people who are immigrants to Canada from Iran. Due to the political power misuse of a self-proclaimed "Islamic" government that uses inhumane and arguably, un-Islamic methods to control its people, many Iranians have a disdain for religiosity (Islamic religiosity in particular). But that does not include everyone, and at times, that perceived threat and trauma experienced by persecuted people from Iran, may cause a conflict between them and other immigrants who practice the Islamic faith, despite there being no ill intent on the part of the practicing Muslim. Once again, this is not always the case, but it is necessary to be mindful of history, culture, power, and conflict, in any therapeutic or working relationship between practitioner and client.

5.4   Policing Your Own People

Some people of color and those from nondominant cultures have experienced being policed by others from their own or similar communities. This goes two ways: in some cases, BIPOC people will shame or police others from their community to act as "good immigrants"; in other situations, those of us who have developed greater confidence in our ethnic and cultural identity development expect others to be as far along in their journey as we are in ours. Carey Yazeed recently wrote about a common conflict that occurs between Black women (Yazeed, 2021b). In addition, the power imbalances between communities of color due to earned privilege can also be challenging.

Though the Western mentality silos professionals (and the concept of professionalism) as being untouchable by issues occurring in the community, the truth is that ignoring the impact of societal issues and power dynamics in the broader society is likely to be problematic. It is incumbent upon professionals and practitioners to be mindful and aware of these issues and address them head on. *Remember that being "professional" should also mean being culturally competent.*

People of color can police other people of color. Being a person of color does not mean insight into racism

5.5   Cultural Humility

The term "cultural humility" was first coined by Tervalon and Murray-Garcia (1998), who used the term as a tool to educate health professionals to work with diverse populations (who were predominantly not White). They saw this concept as quite distinct from models of cultural competence at the time, which centered a White culture as the sole measuring stick by which people from non-White cultures were judged. In many professional cultures, the standards and expectations of what is deemed professional was first established by those in power – that is, White people. And when people do not follow those standards, they are often deemed unprofessional. This even applies to clinical histories. Disclosing a medical history in a linear fashion is customary, and it is what we have come to expect due to White standards. My work with Indigenous populations has taught me that a patient's social or medical history is rarely linear, and this has been frustrating for some professionals I have worked with. Rather than considering cultural norms of storytelling, patients are blamed for being "poor historians" and often a full and proper medical history is not taken. This is a clear example of a lack of awareness of differences between cultures, and also a lack of cultural humility and a centering of a White perspective.

Any working relationship that remains White centered demonstrates not just a lack of cultural humility, but also a power imbalance. The White way is complacently accepted as the right way, and the ways of those from nondominant and communities of color are believed to be backward, unsophisticated, and in need of acculturation to the dominant (White) culture that is assumed to be followed by everyone because it is the best way.

Cultural humility is about decentering Whiteness

Many people of color or those from nondominant communities were educated in systems and schools, the norms, values, and expectations of which were developed and sustained by White cultures. They too can promote White supremacy in a working relationship by promoting values, beliefs, and expectations about communication that were not necessarily from their culture of origin, but which are now, through professional schooling, deemed the most appropriate way to engage. It is in these kinds of situations that White supremacy is also sustained by people of color, but also promotes conflict and competition between some people of color, who feel some in their community give them a bad name by not being acculturated enough to Western or White culture, equating progress, success, privilege, and upward mobility to the acceptance and practice of White culture over their culture of origin.

Christmas (or "the Holidays") is assumed to be the time of the year all cultures celebrate *something* – however, it is a misnomer. Likewise, the expectation that all people take time off in December to give gifts is a very clear example of the above problem. It privileges one perspective over others. In this process, many communities of color who are not Christian, have incorporated Christmas into their practices, and expect other communities of color to do the same, setting a new norm.

This can and does occur with our expectation and understanding of professional boundaries, personal disclosure, and our belief in God and religion (e.g., automatically assuming that atheism is the scientific truth without exploring the presence of scientific histories of Eastern spiritual traditions). These become the means by which White culture is centered, and must become realigned, to now center the culture of the client in the working relationship, to not only promote social justice, but greater cultural sensitivity. That may include a gesture as simple as not wishing someone "Merry Christmas," but asking first what holidays they celebrate and wishing them well at those times of the year.

5.6   Social Justice Through Decentering Whiteness

Power dynamics exist in large part due to a lack of social justice, through cultural and ethnic supremacy of White cultures over the cultures of people of color. Though each relationship may not be able to resolve broader issues tied to a lack of social justice, each working relationship can identify the impact of that societal context of the working relationship between two people and work to deconstruct those power differences and create not just a culturally sensitive alliance, but a socially just one too. And when a working relationship, therapeutic or otherwise, becomes more socially just, cultural inclusion may begin to be the norm in broader settings, built upon one working relationship at a time.

Patterns of White supremacy are common and well entrenched in everyday society, and they become the map by which all interactions occur in a working relationship. Though damaging in any working relationship, these are especially harmful in working relationships where vulnerability of the client is greater, as is the case in health and mental health.

It is important to identify elements of our current norm that are based on White culture. Since White supremacy and colonialism have existed for centuries, it does not make sense to create an exhaustive list, but rather encourage a professional to be mindful. And that process of being mindful can only occur in the greater awareness and conversation of the differences and expectations, and the openness to consider alternative ways to achieve a goal.

The weight of this can lead many to anxiety, not wanting to center their internalized White supremacy on their clients. This causes some to assume that silence is the better option. There is an expectation in dominant cultures, in other words, White people, that they should listen, and not talk. I would argue that it is not silence that is needed, but rather an open conversation. Silence on the part of any party may create room for marginalized voices, but it can also reduce the opportunity for learning for those who have internalized White supremacy.

This naturally places the marginalized person in the position of educating those with privilege, which is unfortunate and an unfair expectation for a client simply wanting services from the practitioner. Practitioners should be mindful of this burden on people of color and on those from nondominant cultures who simply want culturally sensitive, socially just care, and they should make it clear that no cultural education is expected from them. But also, many people of color, and those from nondominant cultures, have assumed roles as educators, and should they feel comfortable doing so, the opportunity to explain their perspectives may be an opportunity for them to express needs and explain the circumstances and cultural influences that provide critical information for the care provider or practitioner.

Ultimately, to look at a circumstance from a client's perspective is the greatest form of empathy.

5.7   Social Justice Globally

Although I have made it clear that being culturally competent is a local and not an international issue, it is important to understand that local community members often have international ties. But even without those ties, international events and conflicts will impact the health and well-being of people of color in Canada, the US, and in the Western world because of racial and cultural injustice in their own communities. This includes Indigenous human rights violations globally, and matters tied to truth and reconciliation initiatives. Knowing this, and realizing that issues of social injustice, inequity, occupation, colonialism, state terrorism, and Apartheid occur broadly throughout the world, will help you understand that people of color will and do relate to issues of social injustice globally. However, due to politics, fear, and concern about and needing to maneuver and deal with the consequences of psychological checkpoints, many people of color do not feel comfortable sharing their concerns with a White professional. For example, in cases of conflict in the Middle East (which tends to show up consistently in part due to ongoing colonization and occupation), terminology adopted by governments and institutions, such as "terrorist" and "terrorism," create a catch all term often incorrectly applied to all Muslims, Arabs, and anyone perceived to be in those groups (e.g., South Asian people or Sikhs). Similarly, terms such as "barbaric" and "backward" (used by governments globally, including the US and Canada, and the media; Hassen, 2021; Mattoo & Merrigan, 2021), are used to dehumanize Muslims and Arabs, in particular, when they advocate for equal human rights; this situation is not unlike the dehumanization of Jews that occurred during the Holocaust (Gabel, 2021). It is important to ensure we don't simply turn to our governments for guidance on terminology or even ideological stances in times of conflict, as governments by nature reflect political entities and ideologies generally intended to protect political interests rather than marginalized people. But also, having oppressed people respond to accusations of terrorism when they advocate for their rights is not only a microaggression (suggesting they are terrorists) but also a psychological checkpoint that centers your needs, fragility, and inability to hear the needs of your client, and sustains you as the symbolic guard harassing someone claiming only their basic human rights. Remember that at one point, opposing Apartheid in South Africa was illegal, and members of the African National Congress, including now well accepted and celebrated people like Nelson Mandela, were considered terrorists and imprisoned. Remember that prior to Apartheid being abolished in South Africa, there were people in the country who would put Black people who advocated for the abolishment of racism in Apartheid South Africa through psychological checkpoints. Adoption of words used by governments, and politicized to achieve political and even military advantage, can harm your clients. These words create fear, silence, and distrust, in addition to being very powerful microaggressions that alienate and trigger psychological trauma because of their associations with previous harm. As an example, following the events of 9-11, Muslims, Arabs, those who were perceived to be them, and even the Jewish community, were targeted with hate crimes in Canada, the US, and all over Europe and the Western world. This has included hate crimes and murders in mosques and synagogues. In the same way words like the "n-word" used to traumatize and demean Black people have traumatic and emotional baggage, politicized words, such as "terrorist," when applied only to describe one group of people create unfair stereotypes. When used by a professional practitioner, these stereotypes influence the working relationship with your client. It is critical for you as a practitioner to create an environment where a client feels safe addressing global and international injustice. Not doing so will hinder the trust necessary for a working relationship.

It is also important to realize that the privilege and safety (political, physical, and psychological) gained by Whiteness and social position can shield us from understanding the full context of problems happening around the world (e.g., human rights violations with Indigenous people in Canada, the US, and

Australia, and the occupation of Palestine, and the vast and ongoing human rights violations of Palestinians, including the assertions of ethnic cleansing and genocide in 2023, and historically [Amnesty International, 2024; Center for Constitutional Rights, 2016; Euro-Med Human Rights Monitor, 2024; Pappe, 2007; Segal, 2023; Segal & Green, 2024; United Nations, 2023b]), and at times produce White guilt or aligning with a White aggressor (e.g., Apartheid, occupation, colonization). Although many of us may feel we are well informed about events occurring locally and internationally, typically most people only watch news that fits with their own world view (Ecker et al., 2022). Furthermore, social media algorithms now filter news so that it aligns with particular political perspectives (Lau & Akkaraju, 2019), and dissenting perspectives (which are essential for anti-racist cultural competence) are ignored. Addressing these issues creates a tense environment in which Indigenous people feel threatened by simply pointing out human rights violations have occurred, and in fact these individuals are sometimes punished when they do stand up for social justice. For example, when the human remains of several Indigenous women were dumped by a serial killer in a landfill garbage dump in Winnipeg, Manitoba, the ruling political party refused to investigate because of the costs involved. Indigenous people advocating to find the remains of these murdered women were subjected to hate (Bernhardt, 2023) and social stigma because they were assumed to be inflating the significance of the issue or putting the economy at risk for something unimportant (once again dehumanizing Indigenous lives). To achieve effective cultural competence, ensure you are well informed about different perspectives, including being aware of the historical context of a problem and not simply the immediate issue. Seek out media sources from different parts of the world, and different ethnic and cultural communities. Speak with people from impacted communities and communities of color affected by global conflict. Recognize that what you think is politically correct now may shift with time (e.g., Apartheid in South Africa, acknowledging colonialism on Indigenous land in Canada, the US, and Australia). Do not turn to governments or politicians for messaging, but rather seek out information from humanitarian organizations such as Amnesty International or the United Nations. Realize that the pain and suffering associated with conflict cannot be ignored, even in those with privilege, and we must remain focused on the needs of all our clients. For example, in my work requiring me to treat police officers traumatized by suicides of Indigenous children, even though I recognize that suicides are in part due to the damages of intergenerational trauma of colonialism, and a history and sometimes ongoing police violence toward these communities, I have to focus on the needs of the client in front of me. In addition, we must be especially mindful to not ignore language (e.g., claiming "All Lives Matter" instead of "Black Lives Matter," or insisting on discussing "both sides" when working with Palestinian survivors of trauma) as doing so centers our needs, our privilege, our guilt, and our White supremacy, and it ignores the clear disparities that come with problems such as racism, occupation, and colonialism. Working with marginalized clients of color, who may have views and experiences dramatically different from your own, will require you to give up power and privilege associated with Whiteness, wealth, safety, social status, and even religion and culture. Our emotional responses and ties to those conflicts are an opportunity to identify biases and misinformation we carry to be more effective in building bridges with our clients rather than divides in our working relationships but also in our communities and society overall. Remember the skills of addressing anti-racist cultural competence are useful beyond a working relationship, and they apply to our engagement in society as a whole. Being thoughtful about the issues addressed in this section (and in this book) can be helpful in both our personal and professional lives.

5.8   Giving Up Power

Giving up power is challenging but necessary

The solution to a harmonious cross-cultural relationship is about understanding that if you have privilege, it also means you carry power, whether you want it or not. This occurs in any circumstance in which one party holds power, and the other is disenfranchised or marginalized. Though people can always revolt, the process of change and growth happens faster when the person in power recognizes that power differences create disparities, reduce trust, increase conflict, and reduce justice. Because of this, therapists (or any other professionals for that matter) must work to decenter themselves, and share power and authority with the disenfranchised party. This is not to say that people of color and those from nondominant cultures cannot have the autonomy to find ways to gain power; however, the power remains primarily with those who are White. And as such, it becomes the responsibility of those with privilege to initiate social justice rather than relying on those without privilege to make the change.

In professional relationships, power can be shared. Examples include scheduling of meetings at times when others might not be available due to religious services or cultural holidays, using examples and names of people from diverse communities, and ensuring the practices and viewpoints of people of color and those from nondominant communities are honored at the same, if not greater, level as those from White cultures. Honoring diverse and marginalized cultures in a greater way does not lead to reverse supremacy. Instead, it allows for a greater equaling out of the standard or norm to be more diverse; it allows for shared power and enhanced inclusion in our practice.

Examples of giving up power, or decentralizing White culture from those of people of color and nondominant communities, are rare and difficult to grasp. But I find it is helpful to consider examples of what has been done already with diverse groups, that include White people, such as the queer community.

When a practitioner is "gay friendly," the true meaning of that term can be a form of giving up the power of heteronormative culture. To simply assume one is not prejudiced against the queer community, but not be ready to learn about cultural differences between the queer and heteronormative community or to be a practitioner who finds the discussion of topics related to queer culture uncomfortable, does not then truly make one "gay friendly." It means that the practitioner is not actually giving up the power from a heteronormative community and culture where any example of love and human engagement, sexual or otherwise, is seen from a heteronormative perspective.

Health care providers who are gay friendly should be more culturally aware of queer culture. This will leave them more able to address unique health and social issues connected with the queer community. That may also include, for example, working with various relationships that range from monogamous and committed, to open, to polyamorous. Judgment on variations in how love and relationships are defined, centers a heteronormative perspective and not a queer one, thereby placing power in the hands of the practitioner and not the client, making that working relationship dysfunctional and unjust.

Similarly in communities of color (which may overlap with the queer community), there will be specific norms and values that differ from those of the White community, and practitioners must decenter themselves and give up power, adopting value systems, beliefs, worldviews, and practices that are not their own.

6

Common Themes

The contents of this chapter often form the focus of most cultural competence work, treating what should be an egalitarian working relationship as an exercise in cultural anthropology. In this book, these issues come at the end. Furthermore, this chapter addresses these topics from the perspective of social justice, in that the themes discussed are ones often misinterpreted to be less sophisticated in communities of color and in those from nondominant cultures. But considering themes such as family structure, collectivism, and religion before anything else assumes not only that others must be compared with, or measured by, White culture, but also that everyone else is permanently tied to White culture and cultural identity. In fact, culture is fluid and it changes due to the influences of society. Assuming that culture and identity are static characterizes nondominant cultures and the people within them as unchanging, and unable to engage with those from a dominant White culture. Ironically, people of color and those from nondominant cultures have had to assimilate and thrive in White cultures, adopting much of those cultural practices as their own, and it is White people and those from dominant cultures who know less about diverse people in their community and their worldviews and experiences. As I often say in my work with dominant cultures, *"We know about you because we see you as a part of our community, but you don't know about us, because truthfully you don't see us as a part of yours."*

In order for the following themes to be considered, it must be understood that they are not an exhaustive list, that they will not be the same for everyone, and that there will be nuanced variations of these issues. It is also important to realize that depending on where a person of color or someone from a nondominant culture is in their own ethnic and cultural identity development, this may also change over time. The themes discussed below are commonly misunderstood, and this review of them is meant to help practitioners looking to engage more effectively cross-culturally, to be aware of some pitfalls and differences, which may then allow them to work with many non-White cultures. Interestingly, though cultural nuances vary across groups of people, there is an interesting divide between White Western and non-White and Eastern cultures. The latter can often include many Eastern European and North American Indigenous cultures as well. We should ensure that these similarities do not cause us to stereotype and clump large, diverse groups of people into smaller, simpler groups. Rather than assuming that the list and information below is a complete explanation of the person you are working with, it should be used as a guide that would help you ask questions when and if necessary, related to the role you play. These are also themes that you will need to review, learn about, and consider on your own, as you do your own work outside the therapy room.

6.1 Tips to Consider

6.1.1 Professionalism and Self-Disclosure

What many people in a White and Western cultures determine to be professional is often more rigid and cold in comparison with that of many non-White cultures. Since many people from non-White cultures living in Western and White dominant countries have internalized this as what is "professional," it is less noticeable when working with cross-cultural clients in parts of the Western world (North America, Western Europe, and Australia), unless working with recent immigrants, or working internationally. Whereas for professional or White culture, self-disclosure is often seen as a violation of boundaries and even frowned upon ethically as a violation of client–practitioner boundaries, in many other cultures, the absence of self-disclosure is often seen as cold, mistrustful, and rude. In many White cultures, questions about family or personal life can appear to be an infringement on the practitioner's personal space, while for many other cultures, asking about family and having some personal (but not full awareness) of the practitioner's life is seen as polite, necessary, warm, and a sign of trust and consideration.

What is considered professional will vary across different cultural perspectives

Example

I think of my work with Indigenous communities, where in reviewing histories of abuse in residential school, I was often told by elders (who felt less obliged than younger community members to conform to White cultural expectations), "Why should I tell you my story, when I don't know anything about you. You should get to know me first as a person and let me get to know you before I tell you anything personal." So, any information they agreed to provide was limited and shared out of obligation. But even then, they would ask questions about me, wanting to know some of my history and who I was and where I came from before they answered my questions. When I disclosed my own challenges with racism as a person of color, their disclosures were more fulsome, and they thought it necessary to provide support to me. As a practitioner trained and engaged in ethics based on a White or Western standard, this was a challenging experience that required working to balance my own internalized sense of ethics with the cultural expectation of the client.

I also work with people who are from similar cultures to my own; this has included both people of color, and Eastern European recent immigrants, whose culture is also very similar in social expectations. In this case, not only do they treat you like family, they will often ask you to send greetings or "salaam" to your family. In some cases, being from the same community may make them aware of my family, and the obligation to send salaams (greetings) is a necessary gesture to signify respect in many cultures, to those people who are important in someone's life. In this case, the sense of community is critically important. I have often reminded these clients that I appreciate the thought, but I would not be sharing their greetings, to ensure I protect their privacy. In these cases, there was appreciation on both counts: I validated their greeting, but I also honored their privacy and thereby earned their respect.

It is important when working cross-culturally that we prepare ourselves to be aware of what personal information we may be willing to share, without feeling like we are sharing information that would violate our own cultural expectations and comfort level. The need to share information is ultimately, and usually, a sign of respect and trust building, not meant as an invasive prying into your life. Cultures that value family, community, and connection also value the privacy of individuals and family.

As my brother was reminded once doing a medical rotation in our country of origin, Tanzania, connection (or the attempt at it) is often more important than the matter being addressed by a professional. He approached a secretary, and though friendly in his tone, immediately asked for a colleague. The secretary paused, asked him about his family, his children, and his parents. My brother (who had not resided in Tanzania, for most of his life) was perplexed by what he felt was a rude intrusion into his personal life, but he responded, nonetheless. Once he answered, she answered his question about his colleague, but then followed up by saying, "Do you know what TIT stands for? It means This Is Tanzania. And in Tanzania, it is people before work. Make sure you show the same respect to others." These examples remind us that we have to recognize that our culture and our idea of professionalism are not shared by everyone, and we should not impose our understanding of what we think is professional on others.

6.2   Collectivism Versus Individualism & Family Relationships

Be thoughtful not to subject your views of family dynamics on others

It is common for therapists and other professionals to make clinical judgments based on family roles and relationships based on concepts of White supremacy and White cultural expectations. How we interpret family relationships and even family make-up is one such example. In Western cultures, an individualistic approach to community and family might cause people to separate from their family at a younger age and live alone. In contrast, in many Eastern cultures, the concept of family applies more broadly. It is not uncommon for many Latin, Arab, and South Asian cultures to see cousins in the same way they would see siblings, to the point that cousins are referred to and treated as siblings. In many Eastern cultures, parents and older family members are expected to be cared for, and there is a far greater sense of obligation to them. This makes it more likely that homes are multigenerational, but also increases the stress and benefits of caring for a larger group of people. Unfortunately, clinical words such as "enmeshed" are often used broadly to describe cultural standards and social support systems reflecting a collectivist view of community and family.

It is not uncommon for some mental health and health care practitioners to encourage separation of their clients from their families. At the slightest sign of conflict (which is common in any family), it is pathologized in families of color, and separation from family is encouraged by these professionals. It is not uncommon that the victims of this cultural supremacy propagation are children or young people, many of whom already feel like outsiders due to their culture or ethnicity. Further pathologizing their connection with family instead of helping them seek out culturally congruent strategies and community supports to help them retain long-standing family relationships can be grossly detrimental to the mental health, identity, and social support network of clients.

The opposite can also be true, in situations in which abuse is ignored, and for fear of not being culturally appropriate, victims of actual abuse are left with the family who abuses them. Actual indicators of abuse are as a result ignored and labeled as "cultural issues" or "culturally based conflict"; this tends to be a waste bin diagnosis for challenging situations that professionals feel unqualified to address.

The example I provided earlier involving a young girl from a refugee family who was taken in by her White therapist, is an example of the former situation. Sadly, there are all too many examples of the latter situation, where child welfare and social service agencies, in an attempt to be culturally competent, actually ignore indicators of abuse as cultural differences meant to be tolerated, and children who are victims of abuse are left with abusive parents. Gender can often play a role in this as well, where it is assumed then men of color are more violent and aggressive (American Psychological Association [APA], 2017), which is especially common in perceptions of Middle Eastern, South Asian, and Black families (Ewing, 2008). Rather than taking the time to differentiate between what is a cultural practice (which is hallowed ground for some) and what is abuse, many therapists ignore the rights of the child in the process.

In both cases, what would have been typical or culturally appropriate family bonds and relationships were misinterpreted or ignored. In both cases, accurate information was not sought and biases not checked. Regardless of family style, collectivist or individualistic, abuse usually can be clearly differentiated from less complicated conflict, when bias and fear are not interfering.

6.3   Religion

While many professionals might deem belief in God or the practice of a religion to be unfounded in scientific fact, and the practice of an organized faith to be controlling, it is important for practitioners to differentiate their experience with religion from that of the client. Many White people's experiences with "the church," which, to clarify, is based on a European church, is one

Atheism is not always scientific. Ensure you are not being judgmental of those who practice a faith

fraught with tension, for some the denial of sexual fluidity, abuse by clergy, and control of many individual life choices such as family planning. It is common for people of color from religious communities to be treated like fanatics because of their belief in God and adherence to religion. The assumption that all religion and religious experiences reflect the religious experiences that White people may have had with the European and North American church, and the proselytizing of atheism – or as I call it, White atheism – as the more sophisticated and educated perspective is again egocentric and culture centric. For many communities of color and those from nondominant communities, experience with religion can be vastly different and even Christianity may express itself differently in communities of color. Research shows that affiliation with church and community in Black and Latino populations in the US is preventative for many mental health difficulties (Moreno & Cardemil, 2018; Nguyen, 2018). Many commonly held beliefs about "religion" as a blanket statement do not also apply to non-Christian religions. For example, Islam does not control family planning, has more fluid views on sexuality, and incorporates beliefs about evolution. This is not to suggest that there are no problems with religious communities or corrupt leaders, but simply that the problems may not be consistent across all cultural groups.

Furthermore, for some people of color, religion can be tied to an existing functional community, and at other times to a larger cultural group. Cultural interpretations of religion also vary. The wearing of the headscarf for Muslim women is interpreted in some cultural contexts as mandatory, while in others (e.g., Egypt, South Asian), it is seen as a cultural practice and not enforced. It is important for practitioners to ensure their biases about religion are not influencing their judgement about, and engagement, with their clients.

Though some people can clearly differentiate between culture and religion, it is also important to realize that this intersection for some is not so clear in practice. In some cultural communities, a common religion ties together a series of cultural behaviors and expectations. Islam as a culture, for example, tends to produce similar (albeit not always identical) cultural expectations across numerous ethnic communities, including European ones. When working with the concept of religion, it cannot be dismissed as illogical, or not cultural, but the clients' personal experience with it needs to be explored to better understand their worldviews.

With regard to social justice, some religious identities are associated with violence. It is a commonly held belief, for example, that Jews and Muslims do not get along, due to ancient religious divides, but this is instead due to the human rights violations, Apartheid, and land claim issues in Palestine and Israel. But even in that region, there are people across religious divides who share similar cultural experiences and recognize mutual challenges that are not tied to religion but represent human rights violations. Furthermore, Muslims and Jews share common Semitic religious traditions, and there is more overlap between these two religions and cultures than either religion has with Christianity. The point here is that we need to be thoughtful about what we consider to be fact, knowing it may well reflect bias. Information collection individually with the permission of the client can enable us to achieve a more informed engagement, with better and more accurate information.

Many Ethiopian and Eritrean Christian women wear a hijab (hair covering), which is also worn by many Orthodox Jewish women as well. The rationale may be similar, but it may also be more varied and nuanced. We need to be thoughtful and mindful about what we understand about the rationale for those cultures, certain practices, and the differences. To automatically assume that a Muslim woman who covers her hair, an Orthodox Jewish woman who covers her hair, and an Orthodox Christian woman who comes from an east African background, who covers her hair, may have similar issues or wholly different concerns (and your assumptions about your client's hair) may be completely inaccurate.

6.4   Gender and Female Empowerment

Research confirms that the bias toward most women of color, and those from nondominant communities, is founded on the belief that they are at greater risk of experiencing abuse and mistreatment by male members of their family (Van Hightower et al., 2000). An exaggerated focus in media on female genital mutilation in African countries, acid attacks in Middle Eastern and South Asian communities, and women's rights in Iran and Afghanistan (including the classic racist movie, *Not Without My Daughter*) produce a very orientalist approach shaping how many people see women from non-Western countries. They are often depicted as victims, and the men from those cultures as abusers. Though problems with women's rights exist among a broader context of human rights, not just in specific cultures but also globally (Boserup et al., 2020; Sardinha et al., 2022), the complete lack of focus on women's rights violations in Western countries makes the problem appear to be culturally based, when in fact women's rights violations are a problem across virtually all cultures. In the US and Canada, rates of violence against women are at an all-time high. Research on the area of sexual abuse informs us that one in four females have experienced sexual trauma in their lifetime (Pan et al., 2021). Furthermore, in Canada, we have an epidemic issue of missing and murdered Indigenous women; these crimes have largely been perpetrated by White men (Luoma, 2021).

When we approach the issue of gender, equality, and empowerment we must be aware that despite the dilemmas noted above, the role and empowerment of women in many Eastern countries, and nondominant cultures in Canada, the US, and other Western countries, is varied. For example, the first female prime minister in the world was Sirimavo Bandaranaike of Ceylon and Sri Lanka. Many countries in the Middle East have female members of parliament and national leaders. And the general expectation of girls achieving high levels of education in immigrant communities is well known (Inter-Parliamentary Union, 2020). Yet, despite this, biased interpretations of women of color as victims will cause many practitioners to become White

Women's rights issues are problematic in all cultures, not just in communities of color

saviors, rescuing or emancipating women and girls of color from their partners and families, without a full recognition of what might be occurring. It may also be entirely possible that in some cases where abuse is present, the woman is the perpetrator. Social media are ablaze with many immigrant children creating content about being beaten with shoes by their mother. This is not uncommon in many South Asian and Arab families, contrary to the belief that women from these cultural communities are always the victim.

6.5   The Pressure to Assimilate

Systemic racism, a lack of ethnic and cultural representation in media, and the cultural supremacy of White people above all else produce strong pressure for many people of color and those from nondominant cultures to assimilate into a broader Western (White) culture. This can include anything from the celebration of holidays (e.g., Christmas), the adoption of particular clothing styles (e.g., removal of religion-based clothing), beauty standards (e.g., lighter colored skin and straightened hair), a change in family structure (e.g., moving out earlier, older parents in care homes vs. their children's home), and values shifting from collectivist to individualist. Though some of this culture blending is very natural, the shift in cultures and intersecting identities is not multidirectional, and the presence of different cultural communities in a single society does not tend to produce mutual adoption of values (with the exception of food), but rather a unidirectional movement toward Whiteness and White culture. In short, the choices to acculturate are due to racism and White supremacy. Such decisions, supposedly "independent," are actually influenced by White supremacy and lead to self-hatred and a hatred for the original communities from which people come.

There is also a strong pressure from some communities to not acculturate or assimilate, fearful of losing their culture. And so many people of color and those from nondominant communities are often torn between their cultural communities and the larger community, a large portion of which may have adopted White culture. Though each individual practitioner may not be able to really adjust the large nature of this overarching problem, being aware of these conflicts helps them address relevant issues in the working relationship with the client, and at times help the client with choices that can be more healthily based on self-acceptance and not White supremacy.

6.6   Summary

The work to address complex issues from a culturally sensitive perspective, while remaining true to supporting the health and well-being of clients, is not always simple. It requires information, trust, and creativity to sometimes find unique ways to address and resolve a variety of topics. It is easy to adopt quick assumptions and biases, and it is all too easy to ignore important and sensitive issues that relate to culture: I believe the middle ground is the answer. We often blame the culture of communities of color for being simplistic and not open minded (in comparison to western cultures); however, a myopic view that holds Western culture as the best and most liberated is equally simplistic. Culture is a reflection of its people, and people, regardless of ethnicity, culture, or country of origin, are prone to make mistakes. It is in the thoughtful intersectionality of identity that we may find the solution that creates room for a self-determined identity but one that also reflects and represents cultural strengths and origins.

Beyond the Therapy Room

It is difficult to develop competence in anything without ongoing engagement. Ongoing professional development is in fact based on this concept, ensuring that to maintain accreditation in numerous professions, there has to be some form of continuing education. In the same way, cross-cultural competence is not a confined skill confirmed with a certificate after a course, but rather a commitment to a process of learning about ourselves, the perspectives and practices of others, and being aware of avoiding systems and preventing behaviors that create disparity between people due to their ethnic and cultural identity. This kind of work cannot be limited to a therapy room. Given that social issues such as racism, colonialism, and orientalism have existed for ages, both inside and outside professional settings, reversing the impact through anti-racist and culturally sensitive engagement will require the same level of expansive follow-up. In fact, I would be so bold as to say that containing any process of cultural competence to strictly a professional setting or therapy room is clear tokenism and will come across as patronizing to the clients with whom you work.

Given that the professional world has largely ignored the impacts of racism on professional development (some organizations such as the American Psychological Association have apologized for this; APA Council of Representatives, 2021), the awareness of cultural competence and knowledge has remained largely in the nonprofessional world. In fact, many of the words in this book (e.g., coconut, White washing, code switching) were all taken from the street. It makes sense then that the work to remain cross-culturally competent must take information and knowledge from these nonprofessional communities; not just with formal academic research, but from community engagement to learn from the lived experience of people of color and those from nondominant cultures. In the same way that Anthony Bourdain addressed critical topics of cultural perspectives, politics, and even racism through food (the food being almost secondary) in his international shows, professionals must venture out into their own diverse communities, consider those people a part of their community, and with the resulting trust, understand what those experiences are like and why.

The work to remain culturally competent must be implemented by practitioners outside and beyond the therapy room and professional relationships. If not, clients from marginalized groups, such as people of color and nondominant cultural communities, will recognize attempts constrained only within the walls of the office or therapy room, as insincere, not robust,

Be ready to develop a cross-cultural understanding outside professional relationships

and trust will be violated almost instantly. This is not to say that one needs to be perfect right away, but allowing your clients to recognize that you are on a journey to increase competence will signal to them that you are making an honest effort; which most of us appreciate in any sincere relationship, therapeutic or otherwise.

Let's return to Derald Sue's definition of cultural competence as the skill needed to negotiate and advocate on behalf of the client (Sue, 2019). If we consider what it takes to be able to do this, it would require us to have a very nuanced understanding of the perspective of the client.

Put simply, to be culturally competent, we need to be able to understand the inside joke (Abdulrehman, 2019). Doing so can only occur when we are open to, and immerse ourselves in, the perspectives of others, even if this means identifying our errors, enumerating our privileges, and confronting what offends us.

7.1   Friendship Circles and Getting the Inside Joke

One of the first things a practitioner can do is examine their own social circles. Though many of us claim to oppose racism, it is an uncommon experience for many White people to have people of color in their group of friends. If they do, it is usually a single individual. In either case, the dominant culture prevails, and you learn nothing. Research on children has found that the more they are exposed to diversity in school, the more likely they are to move away from preferring other White children (A. Williams & Steele, 2019) and assess friendship and affiliation based on common interests, rather than ethnicity and culture. The same is true for how adults view leadership; generally speaking, when adults think about leadership, they tend to assume leadership is White. But when they are exposed to leaders of color, their perceptions move from negative to positive (Gundemir et al., 2014)). Immersion in culture allows you to see a perspective you might have otherwise missed and is sometimes not caught in research or a book. That said, what will be necessary is (a) an openness to error, and (b) vulnerability to not being the person who is dominant due to Whiteness.

People of color tend to keep secrets about their experiences of racism, or even their full cultural practice, from their White friends, worried about the reaction or not being understood. This can sometimes lead to situations where White friends and colleagues do not have an opportunity to fully understand those experiences which are needed for cultural competence. Alternatively, many people (regardless of ethnicity or culture) will approach opportunities to learn about other cultures, by only seeking to understand surface-level window dressings of culture such as food or clothing. At best, people may believe attending cultural festivals offers them a window into cultural competence. This cultural tourism, however, does not fully allow individuals to understand the depth of what a cultural experience, or the

> **Examine your own social network to see if it is diverse**

experiences of marginalization due to being from a cultural or ethnic group, is really like. Therefore, learning about other cultures will require that you go beyond being a tourist. It requires much more than simply visiting restaurants with "ethnic" food, or only getting to know people of color for the purpose of learning about their culture. We must take a personal interest in broadening our identity as a part of a larger cultural community. Naturally, this is a process that will take time. However, you may find that getting to know people personally, and their community at an interpersonal level in the same way you understand your own community, results in you becoming an advocate for the people you are learning about, because you are now integrating them into your own community.

7.2   Allyship / Co-Conspiratorship

Social justice efforts must be genuine

The word "allyship," with regard to social justice activism, describes the coordinated activism of groups of people to advance the interest of marginalized groups. But critics argue that the use of this word implies a light and charitable sense of responsibility, instead of a necessary affiliation with marginalized groups, working to understand their needs as the needs of part of the community. The difference, it appears, is helping from the outside, versus pushing from the inside, the latter being a co-conspiratorship in which White people see the struggle of people of color and those from nondominant communities as their own struggle. And this makes sense, because it is, ultimately, a human issue to resolve, rather than the responsibility of only a singular community. With regard to cultural competence, understanding of culture from the inside versus from the outside is the necessary shift needed to "get the inside joke."

7.3   Professional Roles and Boundaries

In the professional world, there are tremendous differences when it comes to how far professionals will go to advocate for their clients. When privilege is high, and there is a lack of understanding for the need for professional advocates, it is not uncommon that professional boundaries remain unreasonably high and the client's unique cultural circumstances remain largely ignored. When there is greater empathy for the client (e.g., cultural and ethnic relatability), professionals' application of ethics will vary, and they will find ways to assist and advocate for clients effectively and creatively, while still upholding professional boundaries and retaining strong ethical practice. In the data from the BOB tool, we get similar results. When White people respond to issues that require empathy, there are greater responses to a White man than women of color. When asked who overcame the greatest challenges, respondents believed White men were far more likely to have overcome challenges than any other people of color pictured. This finding might confirm that people have greater empathy to those who look like them, or rather those they deem to be from within their own community, as noted in other research (Neumann et al., 2013).

Issues of inclusion and advocacy that involve diverse or affected communities that are White tend to elicit far greater support. Though we still have far to go to address the inclusion of people from the queer community, the fact remains that a large portion of the professional world has taken to including their pronouns on email signatures, but have not gone so far as to acknowledge and offer days off for cultural holidays other than Christmas, or offer a review of pay differentials between White and people of color, or even work to develop systems to help people pronounce non-Anglicized names more accurately is a testament to this dilemma. We also saw similar problems when the White world rose up in arms to protect the rights of Ukrainians (as they should have), when the country was attacked by Russia, but they remain largely silent when human rights atrocities are committed against an endless list of countries whose citizens are people of color.

Practitioners, regardless of ethnicity or culture, have a duty to shift their world perspectives and their engagement with friends and community to see people of color and those from nondominant cultures as a part of their community. Volunteer with, make friends with, hire, promote, and shop at stores that are owned by people of color. Ask questions, listen, and engage with community members from marginalized communities to develop a more nuanced understanding of perspectives that are not White. If you do this, you will become more empathetic. As Sue noted, you will be better able to advocate and negotiate from someone else's perspective when you have a greater cultural understanding of other cultural groups besides your own.

7.4   The White Savior

Becoming an advocate is the likely outcome of being truly culturally competent. When the value of other worldviews is realized, and when the disparity between cultures and the people from them is visible, the lack of equity in the world becomes glaringly obvious. With those veils lifted, remaining silent about clear issues of injustice becomes unethical, and not speaking up leaves the practitioner willfully complacent regarding human rights violations in everyday life. However, with exposure to other cultures and other ways of viewing the world, the need to advocate for change becomes a necessity. In this case, the inspiration to create change can shape the professional work being done – as it should. But even in this state, it is critical that Whiteness be decentered. Advocacy must occur from the perspective of the culture and the people who are marginalized. Should help or advocacy come from the perspective that White and Western culture has all the answers, it would only promote White supremacy. If in the process of advocating, it is the White voices that remain most heard, there is a chance you will diminish the very

Empower voices of marginalized people rather than simply amplifying your own voice

voices you are choosing to empower, and you will become a stereotypical White savior. This is why, in a working professional relationship, including therapy, your work is ultimately to empower the voice of the client, from the client's perspective – not yours. Furthermore, decentering Whiteness does not mean decentering professional knowledge. This is where the balance of knowledge and learning occurs; where a professional must recognize and feel comfortable with what they know and yet must also be open to the concept of learning and reshaping the knowledge they have, to fit the client with whom they are working.

There was a case I was aware of in which a Muslim woman, separating from her husband, made claims of abuse. In some cases, the alleged abuse was directly toward her, and in other cases toward her and their children. Responding to all of these events, social service workers and legal authorities believed the claims of abuse and assumed they resulted from abuse by the Muslim father, without confirmation or evidence to support the claim. But White saviors, looking to assist and emancipate Muslim women from their stereotypical abusive Muslim husband, completely ignored the possibility of abuse by the mother. In at least three cases I am familiar with, the abusive person was actually the mother. In one case I was involved in treating the adolescent son of a former couple, many years after their separation. He reported to me that it was the mother who was abusive, and my work with other health professionals in the hospital also confirmed that. Furthermore, due to the abuse, the patient who was then a child became incredibly ill and developed very severe obsessive-compulsive disorder (OCD) and eventual psychosis. Due to claims of ongoing abuse that the mother made against the father, the children were no longer allowed to see the father, but the mother continued consistently to abuse her son. She would have him admitted to inpatient units when his OCD (which was a reaction to maintain control in an abusive environment) became unmanageable for her. But when his health care providers made clear recommendations for treatment providing medication and therapy, thus loosening her grip on him, she insisted on having him discharged and returned to her. After I became involved in treating this child, he confirmed to me that his father was never abusive, but that his mother was. He yearned for some control in his life to prevent the distress caused by the mother. In his late teenage years, he began to have hallucinations and a series of psychotic symptoms, and eventually was homeless as an adult for several years, with his mental illness becoming so severe that he resisted treatment. This unfortunate situation resulted from White saviors early in his life who believed the claims of abuse against his father without any evidence, and legal systems which gave full custody to a mother, who was never investigated.

Examples such as this are considered folklore in many communities of color, and promote fear of being engaged with professionals, social systems, and the law. It is common knowledge that professionals who are not aware of actual cultural experiences or those who resort to stereotypes are eager to help; however, many people of color and those from nondominant systems are cautious and trust remains low.

It is not enough to have an urge to help, and it is important to know that the work outside the therapy room that drives the need for change and advocacy should be done without bias.

By attempting to rescue clients, some practitioners do not recognize that they have centered themselves in their need to be the helper, and that they have become a White savior (M. T. Williams et al., 2021). We cannot be looking to fulfill our own need to be a helper or be overly responsive to our guilt because of social awareness. The concept of White fragility, or White guilt, in practitioners who may be learning about inequities for the first time (unlike people of color who have grown accustomed to the inequities) may engender an urgency to help (without thoughtful consideration of how to help) as a means to absolving personal guilt. Sometimes in that process of absolving that guilt, we make the act of helping, more about us and less about the client. There is a necessary balance between becoming an ally and advocate to enhance the voice of marginalized people, and becoming an ally who takes over without appropriate knowledge, as experts sometimes do.

7.5   Jane Elliott

Jane Elliott is an American diversity educator well known for the "blue eyes, brown eyes" exercise that she did with her third-grade class in 1968. Jane Elliott, a White woman, now uses her experience and observations as a teacher to educate, inform, and call out racism (Elliott, 2016). She has become an advocate who speaks prolifically and strongly. It does not mean that everyone of us who recognizes the challenges of marginalized people due to ethnic and cultural identity need to shift professions, but we must recognize our role in either being complacent toward and supporting these systems, or disrupting them; there is no in-between. A therapist, for example, can engage in a positive therapeutic relationship with marginalized clients, but that does not go far enough. The therapist needs to raise their hand and speak up, so that not only the client and their environment can be understood, but other people in that environment as well.

When it comes to being culturally competent, if we do not recognize our role within systems, we are not truly addressing cross-cultural issues. Often psychologists or professionals see themselves as cut off or siloed from these issues. Remaining "professional" to many means remaining neutral, despite evidence of a serious impact of systemic disparities for the people with whom they work. The response is often that I will assist you in this role as long as it does not threaten or challenge my privilege. The adopting of this perspective consistently by professionals fearful of losing their privilege (including people of color and those from nondominant cultures who would have more recently obtained privilege through education) creates a culture of complacency where we ignore the impact of marginalization on the ethnic and cultural identity of people. And this becomes a tokenistic or patronizing approach to cross-cultural competence, where any effective change agent is neutralized with our choice to remain neutral in situations where professionals should be advocating and offering commentary. As Nobel Peace Prize laureate Desmond Tutu said, "If you are neutral in situations of injustice, you have chosen the side of the oppressor" (Ratcliffe, 2017).

If we choose to engage in cross-cultural work solely for our own benefit, we must question our value to our clients. We must recognize that the whole point of being cross-culturally competent and anti-racist is to shift the system. That is where we must recognize our role within the system. That the professional boundary is ultimately about going beyond our role in the system versus simply ignoring the fact that we are a part of the system. The adage, "this is not my job" suggests that professionals living and engaging in a diverse and self-proclaiming multicultural society need to shift what their job is when working with disadvantaged members of their community. I would argue it is always our job to work cross-culturally to promote anti-racism as an ethical practice of any profession. Further discussion on how to do so ethically in any profession may need to occur, but it can no longer be ignored. The role within any system is to use our voice and our opinion in our assessment to determine how we can assist with our professional role.

In an article titled "All Research Is Political," Amanda Sullivan (2021) notes,

> Even inaction or supposed neutrality are political in that they maintain passive acceptance or allegiance to the status quo. Denial of such is a reflection of privilege. Many of us don't have that luxury, but within psychology, many gatekeepers and leaders do.

7.6   Getting Your Hands Dirty

Change requires effort. Ensure you are able to make the commitment

The challenge that many professions of privilege face is a fear of getting involved politically. Remember that part of being aware of cross-cultural experiences is that you often have your ethnicity and/or culture politicized without the privilege of choosing to avoid politics. When a practitioner aims to improve cross-cultural competency, a critical part of gaining empathy and reducing disparity is to see your privilege, check it, but also be able to use it when necessary to decrease disparity. Not getting your hands dirty by using professional influence appropriately, when necessary, signals to the client that you do not understand their perspective, or worse, you do, but choose not to assist. If this is the case, why did you choose to work cross-culturally? "Getting our hands dirty" is often easier than we believe it to be, and we may not realize, we actually do this in other settings when the issue is not as racially or culturally charged or does not threaten our practitioner professional privilege.

Let's say one of your clients has experienced racism in the workplace, but his employer believes this client is just playing the race card. When you meet and assess the client, you determine that they are authentically impacted by the racism, and perhaps even suffer emotional distress as a result. That would be important to document in an assessment report, but it also may leave psychologists feeling like they cannot confirm the racism (despite the client's report) and do not want to get political. If as a health care provider you can note in a report the impact of stress, operational stress injuries, and even workplace bullying, then you can also note experiences of racism.

For mental health and health care practitioners specifically, the need for advocacy is not just political, it is health based, as the impact of marginalization has a clear impact on health and well-being, including mental health (Cénat et al., 2021). Therefore, it becomes the role of health care providers or therapists to note such things. We recognize our role within the system by using the tools we have to assist and help our clients. This might make us feel like we are becoming political, but racial and cultural identities are politicized, there is no other way to approach this other than being political and getting your hands dirty.

7.7   Racism in Police Officers

I work a lot with police officers, and the issue of racism within the police force is ever present. Many officers of color who come in for trauma are actually suffering from trauma based on racist behavior by their colleagues and their leadership, and from structural racism that disadvantages them. These clients meet the criteria for PTSD.

In that case, it is critically important that I mention in any report their reported experience of racism and how it impacts their mental health. I use my assessment of that situation to be able to note the problem for what it is and describe it in objective terms. I must clearly note it because my notes amplify my client's voice.

One of the challenges that marginalized people or people who are not from a cultural majority face is that their voices are softened or completely silenced. When we advocate for clients, by simply noting their experience, we give voice to them, and we add credibility by noting the impact that this has on them. Not only does it make the client feel culturally seen and understood, but we move now beyond a tokenistic approach of simply validating a client and expecting them to continue within the system. We are empowering them and moving to an equity-based, justice-based approach where we are using our own voice to change systems.

The first thing we need to do when we work on shifting systems to make them more culturally competent, to make them more inclusive and anti-racist, is to use our privilege and stand up and say, "This is what's happening here" or at least "This is what this person believes is happening," and as a result, they are clearly experiencing the outcome you will professionally confirm. This is how we take our work outside and beyond the therapy room.

Becoming culturally competent sometimes involves being a whistle-blower. If each of us is silent and careful to not tip that first domino, the chain reaction to help make our professional worlds more inclusive and culturally responsive will not occur. Regardless of what happens after that, we just have to make sure that we are the one tipping that domino, wherever we can professionally do so.

7.8   Conclusion

For some, reading this book might make it sound like becoming culturally competent is difficult. But being a person of color or someone from a non-dominant culture can be infinitely more difficult in a society that consistently punishes people for not being White. If standing in alignment with them to understand their experiences is challenging, imagine what their experience must be like? I had a colleague read a draft of this book; they said, there may be some people who read this, close the book, and say, "I'm just dealing with White people." And that may very well be the case. If you are not able to put in the effort to apply the same level of nuanced understanding and empathy you would with White clients to those of color and from nondominant cultures, then it might be best to avoid this field altogether. But doing so means our definition of community remains limited, and we complacently support racism by not being anti-racist. In the same way that our identities can be intersectional, it is also important to recognize that our perspectives of our communities must also be intersectional. Not recognizing this disadvantages the client, but also ourselves.

As cumbersome as this process of becoming truly culturally competent might seem, it is necessary. And though we may feel daunted by the task of shifting systems, I would encourage us to consider the African proverb, "If you believe you are too small to make a difference, try sleeping in a room with a mosquito." However, I also know that the process is sometimes slow and developmental. And as Maya Angelou (2009) wrote in her book *I Know Why the Caged Bird Sings*, "I did then what I knew how to do. Now that I know better, I do better."

8

Further Reading

Sue, D. W. (2019). *Counseling the culturally diverse: Theory and practice* (8th ed.). Wiley.
This book provides a deep understanding of counseling culturally diverse people, focusing on the concept of cultural humility. It helps the reader gain a greater appreciation of the stress experienced by marginalized populations. Although its focus is specifically for those in the mental health field, this book has relevant information for people in any profession.

Williams, M. T. (2020). *Managing microaggressions: Addressing everyday racism in therapeutic spaces.* Oxford University Press.
This book helps clinicians and trainees develop a better understanding of racial microaggressions as they relate to therapy. It provides thorough information on the research surrounding microaggressions as well as practical skills to use in sessions with clients. The book outlines specific microaggressive behaviors, how microaggressions can be damaging to people of color, causes of microaggressions, how to prevent them from happening, and how to help clients suffering as a result of experiencing them.

Said, E. W. (2003). *Orientalism.* Penguin Classics.
Written by a Palestinian American Scholar, Edward Said, this book reviews concepts of colonialism and orientalism and how the superiority of Western cultures over Eastern cultures impacts culture and perspectives.

9

References

Abdulrehman, R. Y. (2019, June 3). *Getting the inside joke: How celebrating everything helps us improve cultural competence.* Lead With Diversity. https://leadwithdiversity.com/getting-the-inside-joke-how-celebrating-everything-helps-us-improve-cultural-competence/

Abdulrehman, R. Y. (Host). (2021, June 20). Different People: S03E01 (Season 3, Episode 1) [Audio podcast episode]. In *Different people.* https://podcasts.apple.com/ca/podcast/different-people-s03e01/id1504970545?i=1000526200525

Abdulrehman, R. Y. (Host). (2022, January 15). The risks & dangers of Brene Brown's vulnerability for people of color. Bonus episode [Audio podcast episode]. In *Different people.* Apple Podcasts. https://podcasts.apple.com/ca/podcast/the-risks-dangers-of-brene-browns-vulnerability/id1504970545?i=1000547998215

Abdulrehman, R. Y., & Clara, I. (2023, February 3). *Testing bias: How the bias outside the box tool challenges the common conceptions of bias, and who carries them* [Conference session]. Society for Consulting Psychology Mid-Winter Conference, Manhattan Beach, CA, USA.

Abraham, M. (2011). The question of Palestine and the subversion of academic freedom: Depaul's denial of tenure to Norman G. Finkelstein. *Arab Studies Quarterly, 33*(3/4), 179–203. http://www.jstor.org/stable/41858665

Alhuzail, N. A., Mahajne, I. & Khawaled, A. A. S. (2023). Addressing the ongoing effects of the Nakba: Experiences and challenges that Israel's Arab social workers face. *The British Journal of Social Work.* Advance online publication. https://doi.org/10.1093/bjsw/bcad225

AlJazeera Staff. (2023, January 6). *HRW former head denied Harvard fellowship over 'anti-Israel bias.'*

American Psychological Association. (2017, March 13). *People see Black men as larger, more threatening than same-sized White men* [Press release]. https://www.apa.org/news/press/releases/2017/03/Black-men-threatening

Amnesty International. (2024, January 10). *ICJ hearings over Israel's alleged breaches of the Genocide Convention a vital step to help protect Palestinian civilians.* https://www.amnesty.org/en/latest/news/2024/01/icj-hearings-over-israels-alleged-breaches-of-the-genocide-convention-a-vital-step-to-help-protect-palestinian-civilians/

Angelou, M. (2009). *I know why the caged bird sings.* Random House.

APA Council of Representatives. (2021). *Apology to People of Color for APA's Role in Promoting, Perpetuating, and Failing to Challenge Racism, Racial Discrimination, and Human Hierarchy in U.S.: Resolution adopted by the APA Council of Representatives on October 29, 2021.* American Psychological Association. https://www.apa.org/about/policy/racism-apology

APTN National News Staff. (2016, June 8). Negative attitudes toward indigenous peoples highest in prairie provinces: National poll. *National News.*

Babu, C. (2017, January 28). *Why I left my White therapist.* Vice.

Barber, J. (2015, October 2). Canada's conservatives vow to create 'barbaric cultural practices' hotline. *The Guardian.*

Bernhardt, D. (2023, August 29). Manitoba's refusal to search landfill for remains is racist, church leader says. *CBC News.*

Bhui, K., Warfa, N., Edonya, P., McKenzie, K., & Bhugra, D. (2007). Cultural competence in mental health care: A review of model evaluations. *BMC Health Service Research, 7,* 15. https://doi.org/10.1186/1472-6963-7-15

Boserup, B., McKenney, M., & Elkbuli, A. (2020). Alarming trends in US domestic violence during the COVID-19 pandemic. *American Journal of Emergency Medicine, 38*(12), 2753–2055. https://doi.org/10.1016/j.ajem.2020.04.077

Brown, B. (2011, Jan 3). *The power of vulnerability* [Video]. YouTube. www.youtube.com/watch?v=iCvmsMzlF7o

Buchanan, N. T., & Wiklund, L. O. (2020). Why clinical science must change or die: Integrating intersectionality and social justice. *Women & Therapy, 43*(3–4), 309–329. https://doi.org/10.1080/02703149.2020.1729470

Casimir, J. (2020). *The cost of fitting in: An investigative analysis of race-based code-switching and social exclusion.* https://doi.org/10.17615/wmk4-mf65

Cénat, J. M., McIntee, S. E., Mukunzi, J. N., & Noorishad, P. G. (2021). Overrepresentation of Black children in the child welfare system: A systematic review to understand and better act. *Children and Youth Services Review, 120,* 105714. https://doi.org/10.1016/j.childyouth.2020.105714

Center for Constitutional Rights. (2016, August 25). *The genocide of the Palestinian people: An international law and human rights perspective.* https://ccrjustice.org/genocide-palestinian-people-international-law-and-human-rights-perspective

Ching, T. H. W. (2022). Culturally attuned behavior therapy for anxiety and depression in Asian Americans: Addressing racial microaggressions and deconstructing the model minority myth. *Cognitive and Behavioral Practice, 29*(4), 723–737. https://doi.org/10.1016/j.cbpra.2021.04.006

Clark, K. B., & Clark, M. P. (1947). Racial identification and preference in negro children. In H. Proshansky & B. Seidenberg (Eds.), *Basic studies in social psychology* (pp. 308–317). Holt Rinehart and Winston.

Collins, S. (2017). Challenging conversations: Deepening personal and professional commitment to culture-infused and socially just counselling practices. In C. Audet & D. Pare (Eds.), *Social justice and counseling: Discourse in practice,* Routledge.

Collins, S. (2018). *Culturally responsive and socially just (CRSJ) counselling model.* https://crsjguide.pressbooks.com/front-matter/the-crsj-counselling-model/

Collins, S., & Arthur, N. (2010). Culture-infused counselling: A model for developing multicultural competence. *Counselling Psychology Quarterly, 23*(2), 217–233. https://doi.org/10.1080/09515070003798212

Constantine, M. (2007). Racial microaggressions against African American clients in cross-racial counseling relationships. *Journal of Counseling Psychology, 54*(1), 1–16. https://doi.org/10.1037/0022-0167.54.1.1

Cox, D., Navarro-Rivera, J., & Jones, R. P. (2016, August 3). *Race, religion, and political affiliation of Americans' core social networks.* Public Religion Research Institute. https://doi.org/10.1093/oxfordhb/9780199988457.013.27

Curtis, E., Jones, R., Tipene-Leach, D., Walker, C., Loring, B., Paine, S.-J., & Reid, P. (2019). Why cultural safety rather than cultural competency is required to achieve health equity: A literature review and recommended definition. *International Journal for Equity in Health, 18*(1), 174–174. https://doi.org/10.1186/s12939-019-1082-3

Dickens, T. (2019). Managing hypervisibility: An exploration of theory and research on identity shifting strategies in the workplace among Black women. *Journal of Vocational Behavior, 113,* 153–163. https://doi.org/10.1016/j.jvb.2018.10.008

Dollarhide, C. T., Hale, S. C. & Stone-Sabali, S. (2021). A new model for social justice supervision. *Theory & Practice, 99,* 104–114. https://doi.org/10.1002/jcad.12358

Ecker, U. K. H, Lewandowsky, S., Cook, J., Schmid, P., Fazio, L. K., Brashier, N., Kendeou, P., Vraga, E. K., & Amazeen, M. A. (2022). The psychological drivers of misinformation belief and its resistance to correction. *Nature Reviews Psychology, 1,* 13–29. https://doi.org/10.1038/s44159-021-00006-y

Elliott, J. (2016). *A collar in my pocket: Blue eyes/brown eyes exercise.* Create Space Independent.

Euro-Med Human Rights Monitor. (2024, January 13). *On 100th day of Gaza genocide: 100,000 Palestinians killed, missing or wounded.* https://euromedmonitor.org/en/article/6093/On-100th-day-of-Gaza-genocide:-100,000-Palestinians-killed,-missing-or-wounded

Ertl, M. M., Mann-Saumier, M., Martin, R. A., Graves, D. F., & Altarriba, J. (2019). The impossibility of client-therapist "match": Implications and future directions for multicultural competency. *Journal of Mental Health Counselling, 41*(1), 312–326. https://doi.org/10.17744/mehc.41.4.03

Ewing, K. P. (2008). *Stolen honor: Stigmatizing Muslim men in Berlin.* Stanford University Press. https://doi.org/10.1515/9780804779722

Faber, N. & Lei, R. (2023, February). *Perceptions of gendered racial hierarchy differs for Black and White participants* [Poster presentation]. Society for Personality and Social Psychology (SPSP) Annual Convention, Atlanta, GA, USA.

Flores, M. P., De La Rue, L., Neville, H. A., Santiago, S., ben Rakemayahu, K., Garite, R., Spankey, Brawn, M., Valgoi, M., Brooks, J., Lee, E. S., & Ginsburg, R. (2014) Developing social justice competencies: A consultation training approach. *The Counseling Psychologist, 42*(7), 998–1010. https://doi.org/10.1177/0011000014548900

Gabel, S. (2021). *The role of dehumanization in the Nazi era in activating the death drive resulting in genocide.* Electronic Theses and Dissertations. 1929.

Gerbner, G. (1998). Cultivation analysis: An overview. *Mass communication and society, 1*(3-4), 175–194. https://doi.org/10.1080/15205436.1998.9677855

Goodman, D. (2013). *Cultural competency for social justice: A framework for students, staff, faculty, and organizational development.* DianeGoodman.com. https://dianegoodman.com/wp-content/uploads/2020/05/CulturalCompetenceforSocialJustice.pdf

Gover, A. R., Harper, S. B., & Langton, L. (2020). Anti-Asian hate crime during the COVID-19 pandemic: Exploring the reproduction of inequality. *American Journal of Criminal Justice, 45*(4), 647–667. https://doi.org/10.1007/s12103-020-09545-1

Gran-Ruaz, S., Feliciano, J., Bartlett, A., & Williams, M. T. (2022). Implicit racial bias across ethnoracial groups in Canada and the United States and Black mental health. *Canadian Psychology, 63*(4), 608–622. https://doi.org/10.1037/cap0000323

Gray, A. (2019, June 4). The bias of professionalism standards. *Stanford Social Innovation Review.*

Gundemir, S., Homan, A. C., Carsten, K. W., & Mark, V. V. (2014). Think leader think White? Capturing and weakening implicit pro-White leadership bias. *PLOS ONE, 9*(1). Article e83915. https://doi.org/10.1371/journal.pone.0083915

Haeny, A., Holmes, S., & Williams, M. T. (2021). The need for shared nomenclature on racism and related terminology. *Perspectives on Psychological Science, 16*(5), 886–892. https://doi.org/10.1177/17456916211000760

Hall, K., & Nilep, C. (2015). Code switching, identity, and globalization. In D. Tannen, H. Hamilton, & D. Schiffrin (Eds.), *Handbook of discourse analysis* (2nd ed., pp. 597–619). Blackwell. https://doi.org/10.1002/9781118584194.ch28

Hassen, F. (2021, December 17). Stop normalizing Islamophobia. It's dehumanizing and life-threatening. *Pennsylvania Capital Star.*

Hayes, M. (2023, February 4). Digging for answers. *The Globe & Mail.*

Helliger, Jamie. (2022, October 7). This is what whitewashing really means – and why it's a problem. *Readers Digest.*

Hermann, D. H. (2000). Lessons taught by Miss Evers' boys: The inadequacy of benevolence and the need for legal protection of human subjects in medical research. *Journal of Law and Health, 15*(2), 147–164.

Hofstede, G. (2011). Dimensionalizing cultures: The Hofstede model in context. *Online Readings in Psychology and Culture, 2*(1). https://doi.org/10.9707/2307-0919.1014

Holman, G., Kanter, J. W., Tsai, M., & Kohlenberg, R. (2017). *Functional analytic psychotherapy made simple: A practical guide to therapeutic relationships.* New Harbinger.

Horvath, A. O., & Symonds, B. D. (1991). Relation between working alliance and outcome in psychotherapy: A meta-analysis. *Journal of Counseling Psychology, 38*(2), 139–149. https://doi.org/10.1037/0022-0167.38.2.139

Huey, S. J., Jr., Tilley, J. L., Jones, E. O., & Smith, C. A. (2014). The contribution of cultural competence to evidence-based care for ethnically diverse populations. *Annual Review in Clinical Psychology, 10*, 305–338. https://doi.org/10.1146/annurev-clinpsy-032813-153729

Hughes, T. (2022, September 17). *How Alexander the Great became Pharaoh of Egypt.* HistoryHIT. https://www.historyhit.com/how-alexander-the-great-became-pharaoh-of-egypt/

Hui, A. (2019). *Chop suey nation: The legion café and other stories from Canada's Chinese restaurants.* Douglas & McIntyre.

Huntington, S. P. (1997). *The clash of civilizations and the remaking of world order.* Touchstone.

Ilagan, G. S., & Heatherington, L. (2022). Advancing the understanding of factors that influence client preferences for race and gender matching in psychotherapy. *Counselling Psychology Quarterly, 35*, 694–717. https://doi.org/10.1080/09515070.2021.1960274

Inter-Parliamentary Union. (2020). *Women in parliament: 1995–2020 – 25 years in review.* https://www.ipu.org/women-in-parliament-2020

IPSOS. (2020, July 24). *Majority see racism as a serious problem in Canada today, up 13 points since last year.* https://www.ipsos.com/en-ca/majority-60-see-racism-serious-problem-canada-today-13-points-last-year#:~:text=Since%20Last%20Year-,Majority%20(60%25)%20See%20Racism%20as%20a%20Serious%20Problem%20in,13%20points%20Since%20Last%20Year&text=Toronto%2C%20ON%2C%20July%2024%2C,than%20just%20one%20year%20ago

Kanter, J. W., Rosen, D. C., et al. (2019). Using contextual behavioral science to understand racism and bias. In M. T. Williams, D. C. Rosen, & J. W. Kanter (Eds.), *Eliminating race-based mental health disparities: Promoting equity and culturally responsive care across settings* (pp. 99–125). New Harbinger Books.

Kim, E. (2018). The effects of client-counselor racial matching on therapeutic outcome. *Asia Pacific Education Review, 19*, 103–110 https://doi.org/10.1007/s12564-018-9518-9

Lau, T., & Akkaraju, U. (2019, November 12). When algorithms decide whose voice will be heard. *Harvard Business Review.*

Luoma, C. (2021). Closing the cultural rights gap in transitional justice: Developments from Canada's National Inquiry into Missing and Murdered Indigenous Women and Girls. *Netherlands Quarterly of Human Rights, 39*(1), 30–52. https://doi.org/10.1177/0924051921992747

Macintosh, M. (2023, December 6). *"Antisemetic propoganda" removed from U of M as tensions rise. Winnipeg Free Press.* https://www.winnipegfreepress.com/breaking-news/2023/12/06/antisemitic-propaganda-removed-from-u-of-m-as-tensions-rise

Mattoo, D., & Merrigan, S. E. (2021). "Barbaric" cultural practices: Culturalizing violence and the failure to protect women in Canada. *International Journal of Child, Youth and Family Studies, 12*(1), 124–142. https://doi.org/10.18357/ijcyfs1212021 20086

Merriam-Webster. (n.d.). Bias. In *Merriam-Webster dictionary.* Retrieved January 20, 2023, from https://www.merriam-webster.com/dictionary/bias

Merriam-Webster. (n.d.). Culture. In *Merriam-Webster dictionary.* Retrieved January 20, 2023, from https://www.merriam-webster.com/dictionary/culture

Meyer, E. (2016). *The culture map.* Public Affairs.

Moreno, O., & Cardemil, E. (2018). The role of religious attendance on mental health among Mexican populations: A contribution toward the discussion of the immigrant health paradox. *American Journal of Orthopsychiatry, 88*(1), 10–15. https://doi.org/10.1037/ort0000214

Mosher, D. K., Hook, J. N., Captari, L. E., Davis, D. E., DeBlaere, C., & Owen, J. (2017). Cultural humility: A therapeutic framework for engaging diverse clients. *Practice Innovations, 2*(4), 221–233. https://doi.org/10.1037/pri0000055

Nelson, C. A. (2021). The epidemic of missing and murdered Indigenous women and girls (MMIWG) in North America. *The Graduate Review, 6*, 190–196.

Neumann, D. L., Boyle, G. J., & Chan, R. C. K. (2013). Empathy toward individuals of the same and different ethnicity when depicted in negative and positive contexts. *Personality & Individual Differences, 55*(1), 8–13. https://doi.org/10.1016/j.paid.2013.01.022

Nguyen, A. W. (2018). African American elders, mental health, and the role of the church. *Generations, 42*(2), 61–67.

Okun, T., Clare, E. Y., Briones, E., Page, K., & Angers-Trottier, P. (2019). *White supremacy culture in organizations.* Centre for Community Organizations.

Osanloo, A. F., Boske, C., & Newcomb, W. S. (2016). Deconstructing macroaggressions, microaggressions, and structural racism in education: Developing a conceptual model for the intersection of social justice practice and intercultural education. *International Journal of Organizational Theory and Development, 4*(1).

Owen (2011). Client and therapist variability in clients' perceptions of their therapists' multicultural competencies. *Journal of Counselling Psychology, 58*(1), 1–9. https://doi.org/10.1037/a0021496

Owen, J., Tao, K. W., Drinane, J. M., Hook, J., Davis, D. E., & Kune, N. F. (2016). Client perceptions of therapists' multicultural orientation: Cultural (missed) opportunities and cultural humility. *Professional Psychology: Research and Practice, 47*(1), 30–37. https://doi.org/10.1037/pro0000046

Palagia, O. (2022). The image of Alexander in ancient art. In R. Stoneman (Ed.), *A history of Alexander the Great in world culture* (pp. 42–64). Cambridge University Press. https://doi.org/10.1017/9781316711798.004

Pan, Y., Lin, X., Liu, J., Zhang, S., Zeng, X., Chen, F., & Wu, J. (2021). Prevalence of childhood sexual abuse among women using the Childhood Trauma Questionnaire: A worldwide meta-analysis. *Trauma, Violence, & Abuse, 22*(5), 1181–1191. https://doi.org/10.1177/1524838020912867

Panelo, N. D. (2010). The model minority student: Asian American students and the relationships between acculturation to western values, family pressures, and mental health concerns. *The Vermont Connection, 31*(1).

Pappe, I. (2007). *The ethnic cleansing of Palestine.* OneWorld Publications.

Parsons, S., Collins, T. Z., & Cox, R. D. (2019). Race and color in Louisiana: An update on the Clark and Clark doll experiment. *Journal of Race & Policy, 15*(1), 24–53.

Pursaga, J. (2023, January 4). City ponders letting employees pick their own stat holidays to reflect culture. *Winnipeg Free Press*, 1.

Ramasubramanian, S. (2010). Television viewing, racial attitudes, and policy preferences: Exploring the role of social identity and intergroup emotions in influencing support for affirmative action. *Communication Monographs, 77*(1), 102–120. https://doi.org/10.1080/03637750903514300

Ranta, R. (2015). Re-Arabizing Israeli food culture. *Food, Culture & Society, 18*(4), 611–627. https://doi.org/10.1080/15528014.2015.1088192

Ratcliffe, S. (2017). *Oxford essential quotations* (5th ed.). Oxford Reference. https://doi.org/10.1093/acref/9780191843730.001.0001

Ratts, M. J. (2015). *Multicultural and social justice counseling competencies.* Multicultural Counseling Competencies Revisions Committee. https://www.counseling.org/docs/default-source/competencies/multicultural-and-social-justice-counseling-competencies.pdf?sfvrsn=20

Said, E. W. (2003). *Orientalism.* Penguin Classics.

Sardinha, L., Maheu-Giroux, M., Stöckl, H., Meyer, S. R., & García-Moreno, C. (2022). Global, regional, and national prevalence estimates of physical or sexual, or both, intimate partner violence against women in 2018. *Lancet, 399*(10327), 803–813. https://doi.org/10.1016/S0140-6736(21)02664-7

Segal, R. (2023, October 13). *A textbook case of genocide.* Jewish Currents. https://jewish currents.org/a-textbook-case-of-genocide

Segal, R. & Green, P. (2024, January 14). *Intent in the genocide case against Israel is not hard to prove.* Al Jazeera. https://www.aljazeera.com/opinions/2024/1/14/intent-in-the-genocide-case-against-israel-is-not-hard-to-prove

Shukla, N., Suleyman, C., & Khakpour, P. (2020). *The good immigrant: 26 writers reflect on America.* Back Bay Books.

Statistics Canada. (2021). *Census profile; 2021 census of the population.*

Sue, D. W. (2010). *Microaggressions in everyday life: Race, gender, and sexual orientation.* Wiley.

Sue, D. W. (2019). *Counseling the culturally diverse: Theory and practice* (8th ed.). John Wiley & Sons, Inc.

Sue, D. W., Rasheed, M. N., & Rasheed, J. M. (2018). *Multicultural social work practice: A competency-based approach to diversity and social justice.* Wiley. https://www.proquest.com/openview/dfdc0af2f76c0ab4850de741babd7760/1?pq-origsite=gscholar&cbl=40430

Sue, D. W., & Spanierman, L. (2020). *Microaggressions in everyday life.* Wiley.

Sufrin, J. (2019, November 5). *3 Things to know: Cultural humility | Hogg Foundation.* Hogg Foundation. https://hogg.utexas.edu/3-things-to-know-cultural-humility

Sullivan, A. (2021). *All research is political.* Newsroom. Teachers College Columbia University. https://www.tc.columbia.edu/articles/2021/april/all-research-is-political/

Tervalon, M., & Murray-Garcia, J. (1998). Cultural humility versus cultural competence: A critical distinction in defining physician training outcomes in multicultural education. *Journal of Health Care for the Poor and Underserved, 9*(2), 117–125. https://doi.org/10.1353/hpu.2010.0233

United Nations. (2023a). *Study on the legality of the Israeli occupation of the Occupied Palestinian Territory, including East Jerusalem.* https://www.un.org/unispal/document/ceirpp-legal-study2023/

United Nations. (2023b). *UN expert warns of new instance of mass ethnic cleansing of Palestinians, calls for immediate ceasefire.* https://www.ohchr.org/en/press-releases/2023/10/un-expert-warns-new-instance-mass-ethnic-cleansing-palestinians-calls

Van Hightower, N. R., Gorton, J., & DeMoss, C. L. (2000). Predictive models of domestic violence and fear of intimate partners among migrant and seasonal farm worker women. *Journal of Family Violence, 15*, 137–154. https://doi.org/10.1023/A:1007538810858

Vezzoli, V. (2019). Precious objects for eminent guests: The use of Chinese ceramics in Mamluk Cairo: The Fustat ceramic collection from the Royal Museums of Art and History (Brussels). In F. Bauden & M. Dekkiche (Eds.), *Mamluk Cairo, a crossroads for embassies* (pp. 823–842). Brill. https://doi.org/10.1163/9789004384637_029

Williams, A., & Steele, J. R. (2019). Examining children's implicit racial attitudes using exemplar and category-based measures. *Child Development, 90*(3). e322–e338. https://doi.org/10.1111/cdev.12991

Williams, M. T. (2020). Psychology cannot afford to ignore the many harms caused by microaggressions. *Perspectives on Psychological Science, 15*(1), 38–43. https://doi.org/10.1177/1745691619893362

Williams, M. T., Ching, T., & Gallo, J. (2021). Understanding microaggressions and aggression by and against people of color. *Cognitive Behaviour Therapist, 14*(e25), 1–19. https://doi.org/10.1017/S1754470X21000234

Williams, M., Faber, S. C., & Duniya, C. (2022). Being an anti-racist clinician. *The Cognitive Behaviour Therapist, 15*, Article e19. https://doi.org/10.1017/S1754470X22000162

Williams, M. T., Faber, S. C., Nepton, A., & Ching, T. (2023). Racial justice allyship requires civil courage: Behavioral prescription for moral growth and change. *American Psychologist, 78*(1), 1–19. https://doi.org/10.1037/amp0000940

Williams, M. T., Holmes, S., Zare, M. Haeny, A. H., & Faber, S. C. (in press). An evidence-based approach for treating stress and trauma due to racism. *Cognitive and Behavioral Practice.*

Williams, M. T., Khanna Roy, A., MacIntyre, M., & Faber, S. (2022). The traumatizing impact of racism in Canadians of colour. *Current Trauma Reports, 8,* 17–34. https://doi.org/10.1007/s40719-022-00225-5

Williams, M. T., Metzger, I., Leins, C., & DeLapp, C. (2018). Assessing racial trauma within a DSM-5 framework: The UConn Racial/Ethnic Stress & Trauma Survey. *Practice Innovations, 3*(4), 242–260. https://doi.org/10.1037/pri0000076

Williams, M. T. & Sharif, N. (2021). Racial allyship: Novel measurement and new insights. *New Ideas in Psychology, 62*(100865), 1–10. https://doi.org/10.1016/j.newideapsych.2021.100865

Williams, M. T., Sharif, N., Strauss, D., Gran-Ruaz, S., Bartlett, A., & Skinta, M. D. (2021). Unicorns, leprechauns, and White allies: Exploring the space between intent and action. *The Behavior Therapist, 44*(6), 272–281.

WinnLove. (2023). *Civic Pride Campaign.*

Yazeed, C. (2021a, December 12). *The dangers of courage culture and Brene Brown isn't for Black folk.* Drcareyyazeed.com. https://drcareyyazeed.com/the-dangers-of-courage-culture-and-why-brene-brown-isnt-for-Black-folk/

Yazeed, C. (2021b, November 3). *Why Black women hurt each other in the workplace.* Drcareyyazeed.com. https://drcareyyazeed.com/why-Black-women-hurt-each-other-in-the-workplace/

10
Appendix: Tools and Resources

The following materials for your book can be downloaded free of charge once you register on the Hogrefe website:

Appendix 1: Online Resources

Appendix 2: Celebrating Everything: A Guide to Improving Inclusion Through
Celebration

How to proceed:

1. Go to www.hgf.io/media and create a user account. If you already have one, please log in.

2. Go to **My supplementary materials** in your account dashboard and enter the code below. You will automatically be redirected to the download area, where you can access and download the supplementary materials.

   Code: B-E3NF2N

To make sure you have permanent direct access to all the materials, we recommend that you download them and save them on your computer.

Appendix 1: Online Resources

This is a **preview** of the content that is available in the downloadable material of this book. Please see p. 101 for instructions on how to obtain the full-sized, printable PDF.

The Bias Outside the Box Tool

This online tool helps participants have a clearer picture of the biases they carry toward people of color and those from different cultural backgrounds. It can help create insights which ultimately can facilitate change in cognitive and behavioral therapy. Data are collected from this tool, so we can better understand bias (https://leadwithdiversity.com/testbias/).

LivingWithRacism.com

Living With Racism is a free learning resource that shares short accounts of racism experienced by people of color, to develop empathy and proximity to the experiences of racism, so those who do not experience it can understand the impact of even the most subtle forms of racism (https://livingwithracism.com/).

TEDx Talk

Resolving Unconscious Bias – Dr. Rehman Abdulrehman (https://www.youtube.com/watch?v=Jk1e2zCuy_I)

#CelebrateEverything

This is an infographic tip, a part of a larger civic pride campaign using positive psychology to improve civic engagement. This site specifically refers to how cultural inclusion is better for the well-being of all citizens (https://WinnLove.ca/; Celebrate Everything)

This is a **preview** of the content that is available in the downloadable material of this book. Please see p. 101 for instructions on how to obtain the full-sized, printable PDF.

Appendix 2: Celebrating Everything: A Guide to Improving Inclusion Through Celebration

The key to ensuring representation culturally, across all segments of North American society is to assist with creating a *truly* multicultural society. This means that North Americans from all communities feel they are represented publicly, under one cultural umbrella or another. Celebrating Everything, or more accurately, at least one major holiday or observance for each of the different cultural communities in our country, can allow us not only to be more inclusive, but to help educate and inform those who do not belong to those communities, thereby reducing ignorance, and thus bias and the roots of racism. In many ways, this makes us more cross-culturally competent, promoting pluralism and democracy. Celebration allows us to address ignorance and hate, through a more functional and positive way than with the anxiety and stress that typically come with this kind of discussion. The goal is also to celebrate these holidays the way that these North American communities celebrate them, turning what is typically perceived as foreign into local, exotic into normal, and what is other or *them* into *us*; increasing relatability between different groups of people. To be clear, this is different from global festivals where "international cultures" can be stereotyped into how things were or are done "back home." Rather, this is an initiative to shift thinking and practice to local intersectional identity, and what we truly consider Canadian or American, to move beyond tokenism, and to empower positive cultural and ethnic identities in all North Americans, young and old.

Our current calendar of holidays reflects Christian, or Eurocentric holidays, or at least, the primary ones do. The goal now is to ensure equity and representation by doing the same with other cultural groups by looking at the umbrella groups that communities fall under.

The best way to do this is to start to ensure major religious or cultural holidays are acknowledged publicly by government, business, schools, the media, and private organizations. Since religious holidays (not unlike Christmas and Easter) are celebrated both religiously and culturally (secularly) from people in cultural communities, it is important religious and cultural holidays are included in this calendar and they are therefore noted below.

Religious Holidays

Christianity

Communities who are not White but come from countries with a Christian heritage or culture (e.g., Latino, African, European, and Philipino communities), will be included in the current celebration of holidays such as Christmas and Easter. To be more inclusive, considering the different ways these are celebrated by cultural communities and bringing those into our current practice will allow those already existent holidays to feel more inclusive (e.g., Popcorn ceremony for the Ethiopian community). But because they already exist, cultural communities from Christian-based countries, will already have representation. Our focus will be to include holidays listed below, as they are not currently represented. Including different cultural aspects to already celebrated holidays is easier to do, and we do some of this already. Holidays below are where we need to place our focus to increase equity and inclusion.

Judaism
- Rosh Hashanah.
- Yom Kippur (observed not celebrated).

Islam
- Ramadan and Eid al Fitr (month-long observance, day celebrated at the end).
- Eid al Adha

Hinduism
- Diwali (also celebrated by Sikhs, Jains, & Buddhists).

Buddhism
- Vesak (birth of Buddha). Many Buddhists also belong to other cultural communities and celebrate other noted holidays included on this list, and may find inclusion in those holidays.

Sikhism
- Baisahki (Vasakhi)

Baha'i
- Nowruz (Iranian or Persian New Year; also celebrated culturally by Persian, Kurdish, & Afghan communities). But Baha'is also celebrate many Muslim and Christian holidays as well.

Cultural Holidays

It will also be important to ensure representation of cultural holidays from communities that may not belong to any religious community or have intersecting identities that are very important to them.

Two that I can think of that fall in that category and that do not have representation in the religious holidays noted above are the following:

East Asian Community
- Lunar New Year (less inclusive term was Chinese New Year).

Indigenous Community
- National Indigenous People's day. This will be the most important day to celebrate, as it celebrates the First Peoples of Canada and the US, and can be a step toward reconciliation.

Black Community
- Kwanzaa. Celebrated by some people in the Black community, this is an annual celebration of African American culture, culminating in a feast on the 6th day – called Karamu. Created by activist Maulana Karenga to have a holiday reflective of African American culture. **This is celebrated by some Canadians as well.**

Note. Consultation with communities is always encouraged, as it allows clarification of how these holidays and observances can be acknowledged respectfully, and fully.

Peer Commentaries

In this book, Dr. Abdulrehman walks the reader through concrete steps to become a culturally aware and anti-racist therapist. It is written in an accessible way, summarizing a growing literature on the impact of racism on communities of color and how clinicians can respond. His nuanced and intersectional descriptions are in stark contrast to many books that tend to teach cultural competence through a "tourist" lens. The author's use of self-disclosure and case examples from his own practice to illustrate the concepts in the book are especially impactful.

Ana J. Bridges, PhD, Director, Diversity Research and Enhanced Access for Minorities (DREAM) Lab, University of Arkansas, Fayetteville, AR

Dr. Abdulrehman has spent his career focusing on multicultural psychology, helping individuals see the world through a multicultural lens. He conceptualizes anti-racist cultural competence as a way to assist individuals understand how one's race, ethnicity, culture, and experiences shape their view of the world, the way they interact with others, and, for clinicians, the impact on the therapeutic relationship and treatment outcome. Using a social justice framework, Dr. Abdulrehman explains the complexities involved in race and culture in this book. Core concepts and terms, such as internalized racism, code switching, and cultural congruence, are explained in a way that readers can easily understand. In addition to presenting the results of his research spanning many years, he uses personal experiences and examples to underscore his points. His thoughts and recommendations are clear and concise, and thus easy to implement and integrate into the therapeutic environment. Of course, it is not easy to change thought processes as this requires much self-examination and challenging preconceived and learned thoughts and behaviors. Dr. Abdulrehman has kept this in mind in presenting the material. Although he frequently presents material from his Canadian background, experiences, and perspectives, the concepts apply globally. The material covers a range of topics, from basic concepts to characteristics of the clinician and how these impact the therapeutic relationship.

I highly recommend this book for clinicians and others who are interested in enhancing their cultural competence and being a part of a more equitable society.

Jennifer F. Kelly, PhD, ABPP, Licensed Psychologist; 2021 President, American Psychological Association

I highly recommend this excellent resource for developing anti-racist cultural competence. In addition to providing useful clinical material, it addresses important topics such as intersecting identities, internalized racism, and the role of practitioners outside the therapy room.

Lillian Comas-Díaz, PhD, Clinical Professor, George Washington University, Washington, DC; Author, *Multicultural Care: A Clinician's Guide to Cultural Competence*

In a world thirsting for equity and justice, Developing Anti-Racist Cultural Competence *by Rehman Abdulrehman stands as a beacon of enlightenment and empowerment. In this crucial moment of societal introspection, Abdulrehman's work emerges as an indispensable guide for individuals and institutions committed to dismantling systemic racism.*

Abdulrehman's approach is refreshingly comprehensive, blending scholarly insights with practical strategies. Through a nuanced exploration of cultural competence, he equips readers with the tools to not only recognize their own biases but also to actively confront and challenge them. By centering anti-racism as a core component of cultural competence, Abdulrehman underscores the urgency of this work in every facet of our lives.

What sets this book apart is its emphasis on actionable steps. Rather than merely discussing abstract concepts, Abdulrehman offers tangible frameworks and exercises for readers to engage with. Whether you're an educator, healthcare professional, corporate leader, or concerned citizen, you'll find invaluable guidance on how to foster inclusive environments and advocate for meaningful change.

Moreover, Abdulrehman's writing is imbued with empathy and humility powered by his own experiences, creating a safe space for readers to navigate difficult conversations and confront uncomfortable truths. His commitment to fostering understanding and empathy underscores the transformative potential of anti-racist cultural competence.

In essence, Developing Anti-Racist Cultural Competence *is not just a book – it's a manifesto for building a more just and equitable world. I wholeheartedly endorse this essential resource and believe it has the power to spark meaningful change in individuals, organizations, and society at large.*

Zachary S. Nunn, PHR, SHRM-CP, Founder of Living Corporate